IDIOT'S GUIDES.
AS EASY AS IT GETS!

Vegetable Gardening

by John Tullock

D1247316

FEB 1 2 2015

ALPHA

A member of Penguin Group (USA) Inc.

ALPHA BOOKS

Published by Penguin Group (USA) Inc.

Penguin Group (USA) Inc., 375 Hudson Street, New York, New York 10014, USA • Penguin Group (Canada), 90 Eglinton Avenue East, Suite 700, Toronto, Ontario M4P 2Y3, Canada (a division of Pearson Penguin Canada Inc.) • Penguin Books Ltd., 80 Strand, London WC2R 0RL, England • Penguin Ireland, 25 St. Stephen's Green, Dublin 2, Ireland (a division of Penguin Books Ltd.) • Penguin Group (Australia), 250 Camberwell Road, Camberwell, Victoria 3124, Australia (a division of Pearson Australia Group Pty. Ltd.) • Penguin Books India Pvt. Ltd., 11 Community Centre, Panchsheel Park, New Delhi—110 017, India • Penguin Group (NZ), 67 Apollo Drive, Rosedale, North Shore, Auckland 1311, New Zealand (a division of Pearson New Zealand Ltd.) • Penguin Books (South Africa) (Pty.) Ltd., 24 Sturdee Avenue, Rosebank, Johannesburg 2196, South Africa • Penguin Books Ltd., Registered Offices: 80 Strand, London WC2R 0RL, England

International Standard Book Number: 978-1-61564-709-5

Library of Congress Catalog Card Number: 2014943313

16 15 14   8 7 6 5 4 3 2 1

Interpretation of the printing code: The rightmost number of the first series of numbers is the year of the book's printing; the rightmost number of the second series of numbers is the number of the book's printing. For example, a printing code of 14-1 shows that the first printing occurred in 2014.

Note: This publication contains the opinions and ideas of its author. It is intended to provide helpful and informative material on the subject matter covered. It is sold with the understanding that the author and publisher are not engaged in rendering professional services in the book. If the reader requires personal assistance or advice, a competent professional should be consulted. The author and publisher specifically disclaim any responsibility for any liability, loss, or risk, personal or otherwise, which is incurred as a consequence, directly or indirectly, of the use and application of any of the contents of this book.

Most Alpha books are available at special quantity discounts for bulk purchases for sales promotions, premiums, fund-raising, or educational use. Special books, or book excerpts, can also be created to fit specific needs. For details, write: Special Markets, Alpha Books, 375 Hudson Street, New York, NY 10014.

Trademarks: All terms mentioned in this book that are known to be or are suspected of being trademarks or service marks have been appropriately capitalized. Alpha Books and Penguin Group (USA) Inc. cannot attest to the accuracy of this information. Use of a term in this book should not be regarded as affecting the validity of any trademark or service mark.

PUBLISHER
Mike Sanders

EXECUTIVE MANAGING EDITOR
Billy Fields

SENIOR ACQUISITIONS EDITOR
Tom Stevens

DEVELOPMENT EDITOR
John Etchison

PRODUCTION EDITOR
Jana M. Stefanciosa

DESIGN SUPERVISOR
William Thomas

LAYOUT TECHNICIAN
Brian Massey

INDEXER:
Celia McCoy

PROOFREADER:
Monica Stone

Contents

SECTION 2 BEYOND THE BASICS 83

SECTION 3 VEGETABLES TO GROW 115

SECTION 4   PERENNIAL CROPS 221

SECTION 5   CULINARY HERBS 245

INDEX 276

Introduction

From urban rooftops and balconies to suburban backyards and vacant lots, people are growing a remarkable and ever-increasing variety of their own food.

Besides better flavor, backyard vegetables offer the highest levels of nutrition—good news in an era when eating healthy has become a passion for many people. Add to this the benefits of the moderate exercise gardening requires, and it is easy to see why it is estimated that one in three households grows food.

Enthusiasm for a project does not always guarantee success. I find that beginners are more reluctant to attempt vegetable growing than orchid growing. In either case, the varied needs of the different types of plants can be daunting at first, but when you learn to consider the plants in terms of groups with shared characteristics, the task becomes much simpler.

It is my assumption throughout the book that the reader is growing a small garden for the family kitchen, in raised beds or containers and in a sunny corner of a suburban backyard or city hardscape. The emphasis is on obtaining quality, variety, and seasonal abundance from plants appropriate to the climate and circumstances. With a minimum of investment and some forethought, any home gardener can do better with a given crop—say, tomatoes—than 99 percent of commercial growers.

Gardening can be summed up by stating that all one needs to do is provide the plants with four things: sun, soil, water, and fertilizer. To that list some might add a trellis. Over the years, gardeners have learned that raised beds or large containers make home vegetable gardening easier to master. The reduction in productivity over in-ground growing is a small price to pay for less work, fewer pests, and a cleaner harvest.

Those who wish to grow a wider variety and greater quantity of food will find encouragement in the discussions on extending the season, intercropping, and succession planting. Aspiring master gardeners should devote particular attention to the advice given on developing a plan and keeping records.

My own garden is located at latitude 36°N, and I have personal experience with all of the crops and activities discussed in these pages.

How This Book Is Organized

The book is divided into five sections:

Section 1: Food Gardening 101

We begin with the basic skills and equipment needed for a successful vegetable garden. Choosing a location and building soil fertility naturally precede advice on planting, routine care and control of weeds, insects and diseases.

Section 2: Beyond the Basics

Making compost and extending the normal growing season are the main topics in this section. Controlling plant pests with a combination of organic pesticides and ecological strategies, collectively known as *integrated pest management,* comprises the remainder.

Section 3: Vegetables to Grow

This section, a catalog of vegetable possibilities arranged alphabetically, provides clear, concise summaries of the best ways to plant, cultivate, and harvest more than 50 vegetable crops. Suggestions for storage, preservation, and uses are also included.

Section 4: Perennial Crops

Perennial crops return year after year, typically becoming larger and more productive with each passing season. This section covers some small fruits, as well as asparagus, artichokes, and various members of the onion family.

Section 5: Culinary Herbs

Herbs are ideal choices for the small space grower. Many herbs can be grown in a patio box or a small bed near the kitchen door. Growing instructions are provided for 16 annual and perennial herbs.

Acknowledgments

I could never have written this book without the support and help of my husband and best friend, Jerry Yarnell; this year we celebrate four decades of partnership and love.

My grandparents Clarence and Faye Boswell taught me how to grow things, and the food we ate together during my childhood left me unable to subsist on store-bought produce as an adult. As a result, I have been a lifelong food gardener, for which I am ever grateful.

Thanks to my agent, Grace Freedson, for her always thoughtful efforts, and to Tom Stevens, senior acquisitions editor, for extending the opportunity to write this book. Development editor John Etchison and designer William Thomas were a pleasure to work with throughout the project, which they markedly improved from its initial state.

Fellow garden writer Cheryl Morgan, and her adult children Catie and Aric Morgan, kindly shared images of their garden and vegetable crops. Dr. Susan Hamilton, James Newbern, and Holly Jones all helped make The University of Tennessee Gardens an indispensable resource for ideas and images throughout the book.

Photo Credits

All photos were supplied by the author with these exceptions:
page 20: Catie Morgan; *page 38:* Aric Morgan; *page 62:* Peter Anderson ©Dorling Kindersley; *page 67* (beetle): Catie Morgan; *page 69:* Chauney Dunford ©Dorling Kindersley; *page 74:* Chauney Dunford ©Dorling Kindersley; *page 103:* Peter Anderson ©Dorling Kindersley; *page 125:* Peter Anderson ©Dorling Kindersley; *page 131:* (top) Mark Winwood ©Dorling Kindersley; *page 138:* Cheryl Morgan; *page 143:* (bottom) Will Heap ©Dorling Kindersley; *page 144:* Peter Anderson ©Dorling Kindersley; *page 153:* Peter Anderson ©Dorling Kindersley; *page 164:* Peter Anderson ©Dorling Kindersley; *page 165:* (top) Roger Phillips ©Dorling Kindersley; *page 165:* (bottom) Roger Dixon ©Dorling Kindersley; *page 177:* Mark Winwood ©Dorling Kindersley; *page 179:* (top) Alan Buckingham ©Dorling Kindersley; *page 183:* (top) Cheryl Morgan; *page 188:* Airedale ©Dorling Kindersley; *page 189:* Peter Anderson ©Dorling Kindersley; *page 193:* Airedale ©Dorling Kindersley; *page 194:* Peter Anderson ©Dorling Kindersley; *page 199:* Peter Anderson ©Dorling Kindersley; *page 205:* Peter Anderson ©Dorling Kindersley; *page 209:* Aric Morgan; *page 210:* Cheryl Morgan; *page 211:* Catie Morgan; *page 215:* Alan Buckingham ©Dorling Kindersley; *page 216:* Mark Winwood ©Dorling Kindersley; *page 218:* Peter Anderson ©Dorling Kindersley; *page 225:* Dave King ©Dorling Kindersley; *page 229:* Peter Anderson ©Dorling Kindersley; *page 231:* Catie Morgan; *page 263:* Craig Knowles ©Dorling Kindersley; *page 265:* Dave Watts ©Dorling Kindersley; *page 268:* Craig Knowles ©Dorling Kindersley.

Gardening 101

The wonderful thing about growing food at home may not be the fresh-picked taste, nor even the great nutrition, but rather the satisfaction in knowing everything about your food from seed to serving dish. Home food gardening has enjoyed a renaissance, as people everywhere seek to improve their nutrition, reduce their carbon footprint, and increase their enjoyment of food.

Another nice thing about home food production is that anyone can learn the simple techniques that have enabled humans to grow plants since the development of agriculture millennia ago. From asparagus to zucchini, plants have the same fundamental requirements for growth and development. All vegetables, indeed all plants on the planet, need sunshine, water, minerals, and air to perform photosynthesis. Plants take carbon dioxide from the air and, with the help of sunlight and chlorophyll, combine it with water to form a simple sugar, glucose. This process powers virtually all life on Earth.

Growing a successful vegetable, herb, or small fruit garden requires some fundamental skills, although neither great strength nor stamina is a requisite. Digging a small in-ground bed is about as strenuous as it gets. Most backyard gardeners will opt for raised growing beds rather than an in-ground plot, perhaps supplemented by additional crops grown in pots or tubs. Raised beds offer numerous advantages over in-ground gardens, despite their tendency to dry out more quickly. Raised beds also heat up faster in spring and cool down sooner in autumn. Nevertheless, the ability to provide perfect drainage, a suitable growing medium, and a weed-free environment make raised beds superior to other methods.

Once you have chosen a suitable spot and installed raised beds, the real fun can begin. Sowing seeds, planting transplants, thinning plants, watering, weeding, and adding fertilizer are the chief tasks involved. All can be accomplished in an hour or two per week, and you have the satisfaction of seeing tiny seeds grow into the familiar lettuce and tomatoes.

Plants that receive proper care seldom have problems, but if despite your best efforts your plants are attacked by insects or disease, the available remedies are easy to apply.

In short, growing food at home is no more of a challenge than painting a bedroom, and a lot more fun. Let's get growing!

What Vegetables Need

Each spring, the garden center benches overflowing with healthy plants tempt a new group of gardeners to try growing vegetables. Unfortunately, too often these attempts have not been preceded by a thinking-through of what the project will actually entail. That is a shame, because with just a little attention paid to what vegetables need to survive and thrive, anyone can grow an abundance of food at home.

The four basic vegetable requirements are sun, water, soil, and air. Each is essential to the process of photosynthesis that is the basis for all plant growth and the production of the leaves, shoots, roots, and fruits that we consume.

Having a successful vegetable garden also requires bringing some creativity to the project. Vegetables need not be grown apart from ornamental plants. The "vegetable patch out back" with plants arranged in long, neat rows

has largely given way to raised beds, vertical gardens, and containers, at least for people who don't live in rural areas. The new trend toward small-space vegetable gardening has prompted plant breeders to come up with new varieties that are compact while retaining productivity, flavor, and nutritional value. As a result, vegetables, herbs, and small fruits appear as integrated elements of foundation beds and streetside plantings that formerly would have been given over solely to flowers.

However, such integration does not happen by accident. You need a plan to guide you, especially for the first year or two. Some vegetables need a permanent spot in the garden, for example, while others must be replanted anew each season. You will have a certain number of beds, containers, or spots in the ornamental garden that can accommodate them. Creating a food garden plan helps you meet the needs of your kitchen within the confines of your available growing space.

Once the garden is planned and planted, it will need regular maintenance. Containers, in particular, need regular irrigation, weeds will have to be prevented from overwhelming your crops, and bugs must be kept at bay. Many crops need regular feeding, too, in order to feed you when they have matured.

In the pages that follow, every attempt has been made to explain the process of planning, planting, and growing a food garden as simply and easily as possible. Use this advice to make your home food garden a pleasure and a passion for the whole family.

Sun

The energy from sunlight provides all the energy for plant productivity. Exposure to sun is thus the most important factor in producing vegetables at home. Ideally, the vegetable garden will be exposed to the sun from dawn to dusk, but in any case it should receive at least eight hours of sun daily during the growing season.

In hot summer regions, afternoon shade is preferable for certain heat-sensitive crops, but as a rule, growing areas should receive no shade.

Some vegetables will produce a crop with four to six hours of sun, although productivity will be reduced. These include:

- Lettuce, mustards, and other leafy greens
- Green onions and chives
- Parsley, cilantro, and chervil
- Green beans
- Mints

A few crops will perform with partial shade all day. They are:

- Chervil
- Miner's lettuce
- Corn salad
- Chives

On the scale of the outdoor garden, there exists no economical substitute for sunlight. Therefore, its availability should be your first consideration in locating your vegetable bed, berry patch, and herb garden. You can import water, soil, and nutrients, but not the sun.

One way to cope with reduced availability of sunlight is to grow so-called "early" versions of crops of interest. These are cultivars bred to mature a crop in less time than is normal for the plant in question. *Cultivar* is a contraction of *cultivated variety* and is a way to distinguish different forms of the same plant, based on their appearance or use when cultivated.

For example, most tomato varieties require about 90 days or more after transplanting in order to produce a crop. Early tomato cultivars mature about a month earlier. What this means, technically, is that the early cultivar is capable of maturing a crop with fewer total hours of solar input than the standard cultivar. Therefore, if the early cultivar is grown with six hours of sun, it can produce a crop but in a longer time period, perhaps 75 days, depending upon the weather and other factors.

Early cultivars exist for potatoes, beans, peppers, and numerous other crops. They offer a way forward to gardeners without enough sun for a traditional garden, but who nevertheless want the nutrition and taste of homegrown food.

Soil

The soil in your garden will be the source of all the nutrients plants need for growth. Plants require three major elements: nitrogen, phosphorus, and potassium, and the element in shortest supply is nitrogen. Discussions of soil fertility usually refer to the amount of nitrogen available.

Soil must also have the correct physical characteristics to support plant growth. It must retain a sufficient amount of water to supply the plants' needs, while maintaining enough air space so that roots can obtain vital oxygen.

The best vegetable gardening soil is loam, a mixture of approximately equal parts of sand, organic matter, and nutrient-binding clay. For backyard gardening, numerous materials exist that change the condition of the existing soil to better meet the needs of the plants. These materials are collectively called *soil amendments,* and their use is referred to as "amending the soil." Just as amending a law changes its characteristics, amending your soil will make it more likely to produce top crops.

Soil that is too alkaline can be remedied by the application of sulfur.

Heavy clay soils that compact like this are unsuitable for vegetables without amendment.

The most common soil amendments used by home gardeners are sand, various types of compost, shredded or ground bark, sulfur, ground limestone, greensand, rock phosphate, bone meal, blood meal, cottonseed meal, and peat moss. Sand, compost, bark, and peat are used to alter the physical characteristics of the soil, while the other elements change the soil chemistry.

Most vegetables require the pH of the soil to be near neutral. The pH scale is a measure of the degree of acidity or alkalinity of a substance and ranges from 1 (extremely acidic) to 14 (extremely alkaline). A pH of 7.0 indicates a neutral substance. A few vegetables prefer a slightly acidic pH of 6.0, and another small group prefers an alkaline range of about 7.5. The vast majority of gardens will thrive at neutral pH.

If the soil is naturally acidic, ground limestone is added to increase the pH. If the soil needs acidifying, sulfur can be added. These amendments must be undertaken with the assistance of a soil pH test kit, and should be carried out in the autumn before the first spring planting.

Many gardeners who grow vegetables in raised beds simply purchase a growing mix formulated to meet the needs of vegetables. This is a more expensive approach than amending the native soil, but it provides relatively foolproof results in the fastest possible time.

Adding organic matter is the best way to improve heavy clay or loose sandy soils.

Soil Building

All gardeners should form the habit of adding compost or other organic matter to growing beds at least annually. This is the best way to keep them rich and productive.

Nitrogen

Nitrogen is essential to a variety of processes related to plant growth. It is also the nutrient in most limited supply in nature. Atmospheric nitrogen gas must be "fixed" in a chemical form that is accessible to plants, usually nitrate. This can be accomplished by the action of beneficial soil bacteria, through relatively rare natural processes like volcanic activity, and through artificial means. For vegetable gardens, most people prefer "organic" sources of nitrogen. These include industrial by-products, such as blood meal and cottonseed meal, composted animal manures, earthworm castings, and various others.

Sand can be added to growing beds and pots to improve drainage.

Phosphorus

Phosphorus is a key component of what might be called a plant's "energy management system." In addition, phosphorus contributes to healthy root development. Phosphate rock obtained from natural deposits is the most commonly available phosphorus source. Eggshells and banana peels also contain significant amounts of phosphorus. When these materials decompose, the phosphorus becomes available to plants. Bone meal, a by-product of meat production, also supplies phosphorus, but some gardeners may object to using the product if they do not eat meat. These same gardeners will not use blood meal as a nitrogen source, either.

Potassium

Assisting in regulating the uptake of water and nutrients by plant cells, potassium is important for flowering and fruit production. Greensand, a mineral, is a widely available natural source. Kelp meal and wood ashes also contain significant amounts of potassium. Kelp meal can be added directly to the soil where plants are growing. Wood ashes should be mixed with about 10 times their volume of compost before use. Otherwise, the ashes may raise the soil pH too much.

Water

The availability of abundant water is essential to vegetable crop production. Your food garden should receive approximately 1 inch (2.5 cm) per week of precipitation or the equivalent irrigation.

The amount of water needed for even a small garden can be significant. One inch of rain over 100 square feet (30.5 square meters) of growing area equals a little over 60 gallons (227 L) of water. Irrigation can be a significant expense. In some regions, it is the major cost associated with farming.

The most obvious water management strategy involves avoiding the use of water you must pay for, and instead getting the most benefit from the rainfall you receive. Several techniques can help achieve this.

Trapping roof runoff with a rain barrel conserves water and makes it available when the weather is dry.

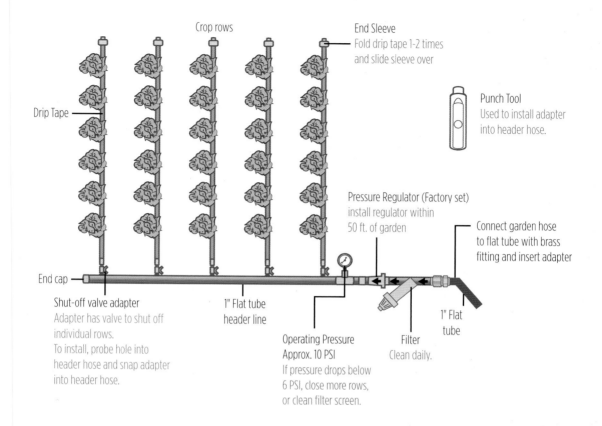

Crop rows

End Sleeve
Fold drip tape 1-2 times
and slide sleeve over

Punch Tool
Used to install adapter
into header hose.

Drip Tape

Pressure Regulator (Factory set)
install regulator within
50 ft. of garden

Connect garden hose
to flat tube with brass
fitting and insert adapter

End cap

Shut-off valve adapter
Adapter has valve to shut off
individual rows.
To install, probe hole into
header hose and snap adapter
into header hose.

1" Flat tube
header line

Operating Pressure
Approx. 10 PSI
If pressure drops below
6 PSI, close more rows,
or clean filter screen.

Filter
Clean daily.

**1" Flat
tube**

Rain barrels are one way to capture excess rain water and store it for irrigation during the next dry spell. The larger the roof surface shedding water to the downspout, the larger your rain barrel must be. If at all possible, a rain barrel should be elevated above the level of the garden, to allow water to reach the garden by gravity via a hose attached to a bib at the bottom of the barrel. The barrel should be tightly covered to prevent access by mosquitoes, and, if possible, shaded for most of the day so you will not inadvertently scald your plants with solar-heated water.

Drip irrigation is one method to irrigate effectively while using less tap water. It requires some additional plumbing, but the added cost will be quickly recouped in areas where water is expensive. Drip irrigation systems all work basically the same way: water is delivered, slowly and continuously, directly to the soil around the plant roots by a system of plastic pipes.

Even if you water with an old-fashioned watering can, you can conserve water. Apply water directly to the roots of the plant, rather than "raining" down on the foliage. Water either early or late in the day, when cooler temperatures will slow evaporation.

If you must use an overhead sprinkler for irrigation, put the hose on a timer to avoid accidentally flooding the garden should you forget the sprinkler is running.

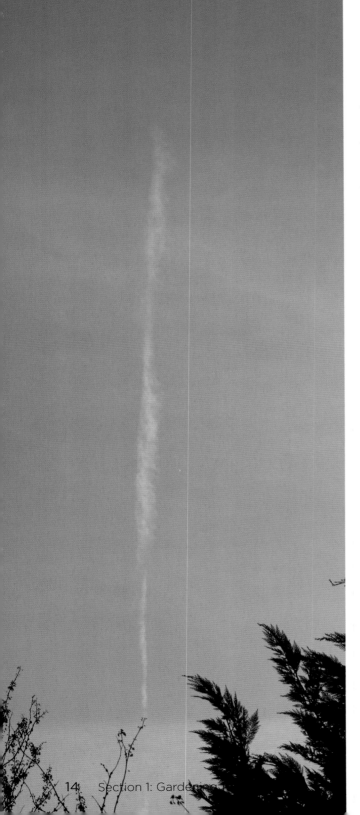

Air

Air is everywhere, and your plants can absorb the carbon dioxide they need without much in the way of help or expense. Carbon dioxide is essential for photosynthesis. Plants remove carbon dioxide from the air during daylight hours. At night, they absorb oxygen, just as animals do. Access to air, by the roots as well as leaves, is therefore critically important.

Growing areas for vegetables must be well drained. This means the soil recovers aeration quickly after being flooded. Water standing in an area 24 hours after rainfall stops indicates that area is poorly drained. Raised growing beds, especially if they have been filled with a properly formulated garden loam, have excellent drainage. This is one reason they have become so popular for growing vegetables.

Good air circulation around plants is an important consideration. If plants are too crowded, air circulation around them is impeded. This prevents leaves from drying off properly. Still air allows fungal spores to settle on leaves, rather than be cast further afield by the wind. These conditions encourage fungi to begin growing on leaves and fruits.

Beginning gardeners sometimes make the mistake of assuming that productivity can be increased by closer spacing of the plants. Crowding is more likely to have the opposite effect, lowering productivity by encouraging disease and, secondarily, as a result of plants shading each other. Follow the guidelines given on seed packets and in catalogs for proper spacing of plants. Most seed companies recommend spacing between rows and spacing within rows. When growing vegetables in raised beds, use the within-row spacing recommendations, and keep plants the appropriate distance apart in each direction. Row spacing is determined by the need to access crops grown in rows, either for cultivation or harvest.

Air circulation is one thing, but wind is another. Wind causes the soil to dry out faster than it otherwise would. Windy garden spaces are more susceptible to frost damage when the wind accompanies cold temperatures. And, of course, wind can topple trellises and tall plants alike. It is a good idea to have the garden sheltered in some way from the prevailing winds. Trees, hedges, fences, walls, or adjacent buildings can all provide shelter.

A garden completely enclosed by a wall, hedge, or tall fence is not only protected from wind, but may gain as much as 3° to 5°F (2° to 3°C) of frost protection as a result of the enclosure. However, the structure must be sufficiently far from the growing beds so as not to shade them.

Good air circulation is desirable, but protect the garden from high winds.

Choosing a Garden Spot

As explained earlier, the food garden area should receive as much sun as possible. The location should be sheltered from prevailing winds and should not be in a low-lying spot where water will stand after rains. Ideally, the grade will slope gently away from the garden area and not at so steep an incline as to encourage erosion.

To facilitate the installation of beds, whether raised or in-ground, the garden site should be level.

If you wish to include perennial vegetables and herbs, a berry patch, or any element that will be a permanent feature of the growing space, first decide where they will go and how much space they will require. Allocate the remaining space to beds for the annual crops. Also allow room for flowers. Not solely ornamental, plantings of flowers offer ecological benefits by attracting pollinators that will visit your vegetables, along with insect predators that help to control garden pests. Include edible flowers, as described in a later section.

Your garden should be located convenient to a supply of water for irrigation purposes. If you have room, a small fountain, pond, or even a birdbath is a welcome addition to the vegetable garden, because birds will be attracted to the sight and sound of water, and will then feed on grubs and beetles intent on consuming your vegetable plants.

Your garden should be readily accessible from the kitchen, permitting the cook to run out for a handful of fresh parsley or a ripe tomato without too much inconvenience. If the garden can be easily seen from the house, you are less likely to ignore or postpone chores.

Your garden should be inaccessible to dogs and cats, which should be prevented from digging or relieving themselves anywhere in the vegetable patch. Repellents are available, although a simple picket fence will deter all but the largest dogs. Cats are more of a problem to fence out. Fortunately, in most urban and suburban areas leash laws and animal control officers prevent wholesale invasions of stray animals.

In some areas, wildlife can be a problem. Deer and rabbits can devastate a vegetable garden overnight. Their presence will require a sturdy fence to prevent access. Rabbit fences should extend 1 foot (30.5 cm) below the soil surface to prevent the marauders from burrowing under.

Avoid placing the garden in areas that remain flooded hours after a rain.

Slope, shade and tree roots all make this a poor site for a vegetable garden.

Planning Your Garden

Start small. This is the best advice for any beginning vegetable gardener. For your first effort, build only one to four raised beds, each about 20 to 25 square feet (6 to 7.5 square meters). The size of the site you have chosen will of course determine how many beds you can accommodate and whether you have room for a separate patch of berries or asparagus.

Next, decide what your family will most enjoy eating from the garden. Make this the topic of a family discussion.

Create a list of 6 to 10 crops you want to grow. Using the information found in the "Quick Facts" for each of the vegetables in this book, separate your list into cool season versus warm season crops. Depending upon the length of the growing season and the general climate in your area, you may be able to follow a cool season crop with a warm season one, and, in turn, plant another cool season crop for fall or winter growth. For this reason, in most areas of the temperate zone, you do not need a separate bed for each individual crop. One bed can produce different crops at different times of the year. This is known as *succession planting*.

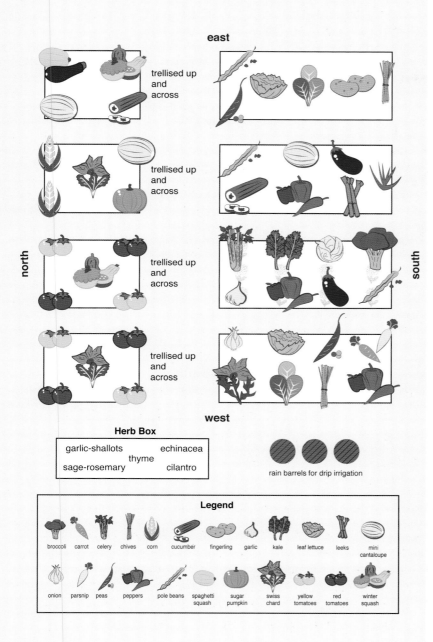

east

trellised up and across

trellised up and across

north

trellised up and across

south

trellised up and across

west

Herb Box

garlic-shallots		echinacea
	thyme	
sage-rosemary		cilantro

rain barrels for drip irrigation

Legend

broccoli · carrot · celery · chives · corn · cucumber · fingerling · garlic · kale · leaf lettuce · leeks · mini cantaloupe

onion · parsnip · peas · peppers · pole beans · spaghetti squash · sugar pumpkin · swiss chard · yellow tomatoes · red tomatoes · winter squash

A garden plan need not be overly complicated, but should include each planting location and utilities such as a rain barrel or a compost bin.

A simple garden plan could include three beds, each home to two vegetable crops for a season. In the cool season, for example, you might grow peas and spinach in one bed, cabbage and beets in the second bed, and potatoes in the third bed. When the season warms up, replace the peas with cucumbers and the spinach with carrots. Replace the cabbage and beets with tomatoes and peppers. Plant beans where the potatoes grew. This simple plan demonstrates *crop rotation,* discussed later in the book, as well as succession planting.

It is helpful to visualize your plan with a sketch. This can be accomplished easily with graph paper, a ruler, and a pencil. Numerous online resources and phone or tablet apps are available to facilitate creation of more complex plans. Digital planning software often features a gardening database that automatically calculates days to maturity and so forth. As long as you have some guidance as to how your gardening effort should proceed, the exact format of your garden plan is up to you. Many people create a plan and save it, either on paper or digitally, to form the basis of a garden journal. We will have more to say about garden journals in a subsequent section.

Vegetables in Containers

Many vegetables, strawberries, and even dwarf fruit and nut trees can be cultivated in containers. Container gardening allows apartment dwellers and others with limited space to produce food on a patio, balcony, or windowsill. Anywhere you have at least six hours of daily sun will yield a crop if you select both plants and containers with care.

Potting Mix

Having the right growing medium is the key to successful container growing. The medium for vegetables should be well drained, yet moisture retentive. Many experienced gardeners rely on their homemade compost, mixed with other components, for container growing. If you do not have enough compost to fill all your pots, you can make a good growing mix by combining equal parts of the following:

- Horticultural peat
- Sand or Perlite
- Partially composted pine bark

All these components are commercially available. Perlite is preferable to sand because of its much lighter weight, but it has the disadvantage of floating to the top of the pot when plants are watered.

Containers

When choosing containers for vegetables, larger is always better. All types of plant containers sold in garden centers will work for vegetable gardening. If the containers will need to be moved during the season, for example, to take advantage of shifting patterns of shade as the season progresses, choose lightweight materials, such as plastic, coated plastic foam, or wood. Terra cotta, ceramic, and stone containers, if large enough for most vegetables, are heavy and cumbersome when filled with growing mix and soaking wet.

Among the cheapest containers available for vegetable gardening are plastic 3- and 5-gallon (11.5-liter and 19-liter) buckets. They are sometimes available for free from restaurants that receive food ingredients packed in them, or you can purchase them from a hardware supplier. Drill several $1/4$-inch-diameter (6.35-mm) holes in the bottom of each bucket before filling with growing medium. Three gallons is large enough for compact-growing lettuces, herbs, and radishes. Use a 5-gallon bucket for a determinate tomato, a mixed greens garden, or a trellis with snow peas.

Container gardens dry out much faster than even raised beds do. Daily watering may be necessary in hot weather. Test for moisture by sticking your forefinger into the potting mix. If it feels dry at a depth greater than the first joint of your finger, it is time to irrigate. Soil conditioner made from polyacrylamide gels can significantly increase soil water retention without adding anything toxic to the growing mix.

Herbs in Containers

Many varieties of herbs make excellent choices for container growing. Perennial herbs, such as rosemary, thymes, tarragon, and sage, may actually thrive better in containers than they do in the ground, depending upon soil conditions. Tender herbs like basil, if grown in containers, can be relocated if frost threatens. For growing indoors, many herbs can be successfully grown in containers on a sunny windowsill, or under bright artificial light.

Terra cotta pots provide good aeration and drainage, beneficial to all herbs, along with creating a rustic look. Glazed or painted containers offer a more festive look, and plastic containers of all types can be used. Lighter-weight containers may tip over in wind, if used outdoors, and thus should be anchored or sheltered by some means. However, the choice of container material is arbitrary. Of greater importance is matching the size of the container to the size of the plant.

If you expect to cut reasonable quantities of perennial culinary herbs, choose a container at least 12 inches (30.5 cm) in diameter, and preferably larger. Ideal container sizes for the herbs discussed in this book are as follows:

Five Gallons

- Ginger
- Lemon Verbena
- Lemongrass
- Mixed plantings
- Sage
- Tarragon

Three Gallons

- Basil, large cultivars
- Dill
- Mixed plantings
- Rosemary

Twelve-Inch Pot

- Basil, compact cultivars
- Chervil
- Chives
- Cilantro
- Mints
- Oregano
- Parsley
- Thymes

Adaptable to Smaller Pots

- Basil, miniature cultivars
- Chervil
- Chives
- Cilantro
- Dill, leaves only
- Parsley
- Thyme, French

The foregoing recommendations are only guidelines. All herbs will grow more abundantly and yield more harvestable leaves if grown in the largest available containers. Nevertheless, by following these guidelines, you can expect a reasonable harvest from limited space.

Use a growing mix that is well drained and moisture retentive, as for growing vegetables, for the annual herbs. Perennial herbs need a better-drained mixture. Select one intended for growing cacti or citrus, or improve your vegetable growing mix by adding one part sand or Perlite to four parts growing mix.

Herbs look great in mixed container plantings. Choose varieties that have similar growing conditions. Basil, for example, grows well with dill. Chives go with just about anything, and Mediterranean herb planters can feature rosemary, oregano, and thymes for a blend of sizes and textures.

Herbs in containers will need light fertilization, because watering will wash away nutrients. Liquid fertilizers are ideal for herbs. Apply immediately after transplanting and then again after the first cutting of leaves. Follow each subsequent cutting with fertilization, although once a week is plenty, even if you are harvesting heavily. Mulch Mediterranean herbs with fine gravel and water them less frequently than others.

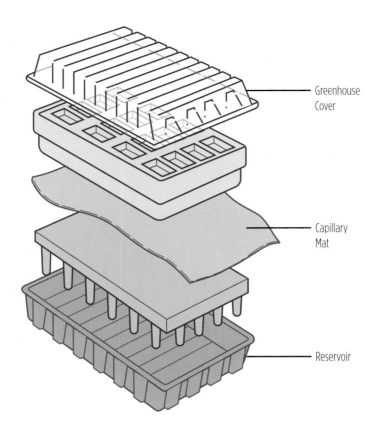

Greenhouse
Cover

Capillary
Mat

Reservoir

Self-Watering Containers

We have stated that vegetables require abundant water in order to thrive and produce a crop. Most vegetables, when grown in the ground or in raised beds, require about 1 inch (2.5 cm) of water per week during the growing season.

When vegetables are grown in containers, their need for irrigation increases because the container restricts the size of the root system. The plant cannot extend its roots in search of additional sources of water. In hot summer areas, vegetables growing in full sun in containers may need watering more than once per day. Even in milder weather, watering can be a significant and time-consuming garden chore.

To the rescue come the manufacturers of self-watering containers. Ranging from very simple to elaborate, self-watering containers reduce the time devoted to watering vegetables to minutes per week. All that is necessary is to keep the reservoir filled, and the container will deliver water to the roots of the plants as they transpire. *Transpiration* is the term for the movement of water from the soil into the roots of plants and its eventual expulsion from the leaf surface as water vapor. Plants transpire 24/7, but at a much faster rate as the temperature increases.

Seedlings in particular are susceptible to damage from wilting. Self-watering seed-starting systems, as shown in Figure 1, consist of a reservoir, platform, capillary mat, growing tray, and clear dome. Keeping the reservoir filled keeps the tray at just the right level of moisture for germination and growth. The clear dome ensures high humidity during germination, and is removed to provide air circulation after the plants have achieved some growth.

Self-watering planters, as shown in Figure 2, have basically the same design, relying on a capillary action to deliver water from the reservoir to the growing medium supporting the plant roots. Systems are available that incorporate many convenience features, such as built-in or modular trellises, and casters to facilitate moving the container from place to place.

For gardeners who do not use raised beds, or even for a specialty crop like strawberries, self-watering containers offer numerous benefits.

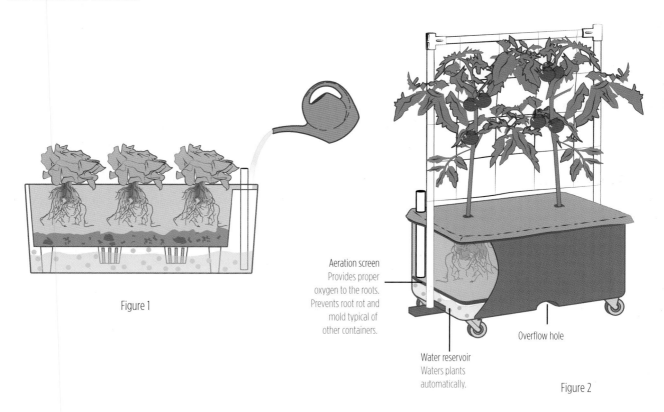

Figure 1

Aeration screen
Provides proper oxygen to the roots. Prevents root rot and mold typical of other containers.

Water reservoir
Waters plants automatically.

Overflow hole

Figure 2

Garden Tools: The Essentials

Tending even the smallest garden will require the assistance of a few tools and accessories.

A watering can or hose is essential for irrigation. If you opt for a watering can, choose a size suitable to your strength. Water weighs about 8 pounds (3.6 kg) per gallon, so a 2-gallon (7.5 L) can weighs as much as a bowling ball when it is full of water. If you opt for a hose, also purchase a valve or trigger sprayer to control the flow, and a "rose" or sprinkler, to create a gentle shower. Tap water pressure is often sufficiently high to damage foliage or wash the soil from containers, hence the need for controls. Use a hanger or reel to keep the hose tidy and out of walking paths.

A shovel and a hand spade are both useful. Besides digging in-ground beds, the shovel is used to transfer soil and amendments from place to place in the garden. The hand spade is essential for transplanting, for getting out deep-rooted weeds, and even for estimating plant spacing. Typical hand spades are about 1 foot (30.5 cm) in length, with the handle being about half the total. A hand cultivator is also helpful in weeding, and facilitates incorporating fertilizer into the top 1 inch (2.5 cm) of soil without damaging plant roots.

A few 3- to 5-gallon (11.5- to 19-liter) plastic buckets will come in handy for mixing potting soil, for preparing fertilizer "tea," and for harvesting vegetables. You will also need planting containers in various sizes if you plan on starting vegetable transplants from seed, or growing any herbs or vegetables in containers.

Wear garden gloves to protect your hands. Working in soil can dry out your skin, and the ways to scratch, prick, or pinch your fingers in the garden are innumerable. Wear gloves when working with pressure-treated lumber to keep the preservative chemicals from getting on your skin. Gloves also protect from splinters when working with any type of wood.

A small wheelbarrow or garden cart will make heavier tasks easier. Moving bagged soil or fertilizer from the car to the garden, or hauling a load of finished compost from the bin to the vegetable beds becomes infinitely easier with the help of a wheeled tote of some kind.

Apply liquid fertilizers or pest control products with a tank sprayer.

This hand-pumped duster works just as well as expensive, gas powered ones.

Garden Tools: Nice to Have

Beyond the essential tool kit, plenty of other garden tools exist that can make life easier, depending upon the size of your garden and your personal preferences.

For the application of liquids, a plant sprayer will be helpful. For small gardens, this can be simply an empty spray bottle that window cleaner came in. Rinse it out and use it for spraying plants. For larger amounts of liquids, a tank sprayer is useful. These are pressurized by pumping air into them, not unlike inflating a bicycle tire. Capacities up to two gallons are the most useful for home gardening.

For application of dry products, a spray-duster is the most effective tool. Units may be hand pumped, or you can buy electrically powered foggers. Hand pumps are best for most small garden applications.

If you use liquid or powder sprays of any kind, be sure to wear appropriate safety equipment. A dust mask prevents inhaling spray, and goggles guard against the wind blowing irritants into your eyes. Even organic gardening products can be irritating to mucus membranes or eye tissue. Always take appropriate precautions.

Although less useful in raised bed gardens with prepared growing media, a hoe and rake will make mixing soil and leveling beds a breeze.

The ultimate tool for working in raised garden beds may well be the gasoline-powered mini-rototiller. It will make short work of incorporating soil amendments, digging in cover crops and many other routine garden tasks. Remember that the tiller will require regular cleaning and maintenance in order to continue to provide reliable service. You will also need space to store the tiller out of the rain.

A small garden shed, if room permits, should be located within easy access to the growing area. Small, ready-made storage sheds are now fabricated out of plastic and are a good investment. The smallest footprint is about 2 by 4 feet (61 cm by 122 cm), but that is sufficient for all the tools and supplies needed for a backyard vegetable garden.

For the serious gardener, a mini-tiller takes much of the work out of soil preparation.

Building Raised Beds

Growing crops in raised beds offers several advantages over growing in the ground, especially if the native soil is poor. Raised beds are filled with a soil mix that has the right characteristics for vegetable production. Elevating the growing area above grade also ensures good drainage, which is important for healthy roots. Crops in raised beds can be spaced closer together than in a conventional garden patch. And using the dimensions given here will make beds easier to reach into for planting and weeding.

On the downside, raised beds dry out faster and will need more frequent irrigation than in-ground beds. They also tend to heat up earlier in spring and to cool down first in autumn. And of course, you have the expense of building and filling them. In gardens with limited space, however, it is hard to beat raised beds for growing vegetables.

For constructing raised beds, polymer composite deck lumber offers permanence, but is very expensive. Naturally rot-resistant woods, such as cedar, cypress, and redwood, are less costly than composites. Chemically preserved pine probably provides the best combination of durability and affordability. Unfinished or untreated wood will only last a few seasons before requiring replacement. All hardware used in construction should be rust resistant.

Materials needed:

- Lumber, 8 to 12 inches (20.5 to 30.5 cm) wide, in convenient lengths
- Corner braces
- Exterior screws
- Builder's square
- Carpenter's level
- Power drill or electric screwdriver
- Power saw

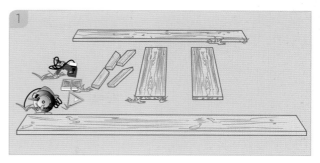

Step 1: Cut the lumber to length using a power saw. If using 8-foot (2.5 m) lengths, cut three 32-inch (81 cm) end pieces from one board, and use two other boards for the sides. In this manner, you can build three 35- by 96-inch (1 by 2.5 m) beds from eight pieces of lumber.

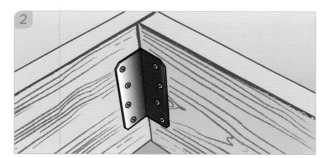

Step 2: Install the corner braces on the ends of both end pieces, using exterior wood screws. Then attach the end pieces to the side boards, again using exterior wood screws. The corner braces will be inside the finished bed.

Step 3: Place the completed bed in its approximate location. Use a carpenter's level to level the bed in both directions. It may be necessary to remove or add soil in some areas in order to achieve level placement.

Step 4: Cover the bottom of the bed with landscape fabric or several layers of wet newspaper to smother existing grass and to prevent weeds from growing through.

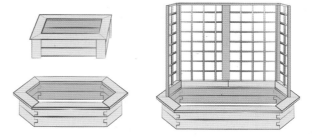

Fill the bed with growing mix, water well, and you are ready to plant! Before planting work any fertilizers, such as cottonseed meal, into the top 2 inches (5 cm) of the bed using a hand trowel.

Plant Supports

Vertical gardening saves space, keeps plants and fruit off the soil, and makes it possible to harvest the crop without bending over. Different types of vegetable plants need different types of support, depending upon their growth habits.

Some vining vegetables, notably peas, cucumbers, and some squashes and melons, climb by means of tendrils. Tendrils are modified leaves that curl around a thin support, anchoring the plant and allowing it to reach for the sun. Plants that form tendrils do best with support elements smaller than $\frac{1}{4}$ inch (6.35 mm) in diameter, such as string, thin bamboo poles, or wire. The trellis material must be supported on a sturdy frame. When the trellis is covered with plants, it will be susceptible to wind pressure, like the fabric of a boat sail. Wood or metal poles are generally used for supporting this type of trellis.

This arbor trellis will be covered in squash vines by the end of the summer.

An arbor trellis typically has four corner posts and is therefore more stable in the wind than the simple flat trellis just described. Arbors can span the distance between two growing beds, thus increasing the available growing space, not to mention creating an attractive display of foliage, and perhaps even a shady spot to sit. Arbors can support various types of trellises, depending upon the plants being grown.

Simple trellises can be bought ready-made, and are suitable for a variety of crops. The pyramid- or obelisk-shaped tuteur (from the French for *tutor*) is a commonly used design. Tuteurs are suitable for peas, cucumbers, and pole beans, provided the variety does not grow too large. They also make excellent supports for tomatoes and peppers. Tuteurs also have a decorative aspect, and can be used for ornamental effect.

Climbing beans and a few other vining crops do not produce tendrils. Instead, the main stems wind around the support. These plants do best when the support elements are about 1 inch (2.5 cm) in diameter, although they will also adapt to thinner supports. Bamboo or wooden poles are the most commonly chosen form of support for beans. They can be arranged to form a simple, flat trellis, or grouped into a teepee arrangement, described subsequently.

A tuteur is merely a decorative trellis, and can be used for a variety of vine crops.

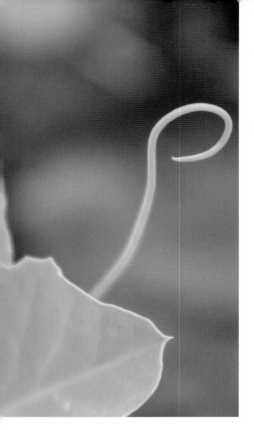

Installing a Cucumber or Pea Trellis

One of the most useful ways to support crops that climb by tendrils is with a trellis made of nylon netting with 6-inch (15.24 cm) square openings. This material is inexpensive and widely available and will remain useful for several years before requiring replacement. The easiest way to use it is to install a permanent support on one or more of your raised beds, using the same material of which the bed is constructed. Make sure the framing corresponds to the width and length of the trellis netting. The netting is typically sold in 5-foot (1.5 m) width and any length from 8 feet (2.4 m) to more than 300 feet (91.5 m).

Step 1: Install a rectangular wood frame to surround the area of the trellis netting.

Step 2: If the bed is 8 feet (2.4 m) or more in length, install additional vertical supports every 4 feet (1.2 m) to provide secure support against wind once the trellis is filled with foliage and stems.

Step 3: Starting at one upper corner of the frame, attach the netting to the frame using small nails or screw hooks. Working across horizontally, stretch the netting along the length of the frame. You don't want it to sag, but if it is guitar-string tight it may break in the wind.

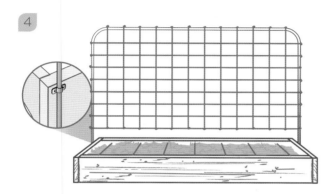

Step 4: Secure the netting to the vertical supports, beginning at the top and working down, again stretching until the openings are square and aligned with the lines of the support. Attach the bottom of the netting to the top edge of the bed.

An Alternative to Netting

Some gardeners find nylon netting cumbersome when it comes time to remove the vegetable plants at the end of the season. If you would rather just cut the whole thing down and toss it in the compost, you use the same type of frame to support jute strings you can just toss. You can purchase a ball of twine and string it vertically from the edge of the bed to the top of the frame. Space strings about 6 inches (15.25 cm) apart along the length of the bed.

An Alternative to Wood

Gardeners who are not skilled at carpentry can make a sturdy support frame for trellis netting or strings out of $1/2$-inch (1.27 cm) electrical conduit. You will need two upright pieces, a crosspiece, two 90-degree bends, and four union clamps to make the frame shown in the illustration. Attach the base of the vertical supports to the bed using metal conduit clips held in place with exterior wood screws. All the parts are inexpensive and available at hardware and do-it-yourself stores.

Building a Pole Bean Teepee

The pole bean teepee is a backyard garden tradition of long standing and remains unsurpassed as a way to grow beans while entertaining children of all ages. Bamboo poles about 1 inch (2.5 cm) in diameter at the wide end are frequently used, but tree branches or long wooden stakes will also work. This project will go quickly with two people working.

When the vines cover the teepee, the shaded interior can be used to shelter a crop of Romaine lettuce from summer heat, or, if kids are about, it makes the perfect clubhouse or playhouse. When the beans mature, they will hang down in the interior of the teepee, and the opening permits you to harvest them. If you make it a bit too small for an adult to enter, the kids can help harvest the beans as "rent" on the clubhouse. On the other hand, with larger poles and a wider base, you can have a walk-in bean garden with plenty of room for a patch of lettuce, or even a lawn chair and a glass of wine.

The teepee concept can be expanded upon to accommodate cucumbers, winter squash, melons or other vining crops. The vines will cover the structure and the fruit will be suspended inside, making harvest easy. Just remember that heavy fruits like squash and melons will need individual cloth hammocks to support them. A large, sturdy teepee should be made with poles at least 1 $\frac{1}{2}$ inches (3.8 cm) in diameter at the base as the main supports, with thinner poles in between for tendrils to wrap themselves around.

Step 1: Lay out a circle in the growing area about 4 feet (1.2 m) in diameter.

Step 2: Surround the circle with the poles, teepee style, bringing them together at the apex. Space the poles 6 to 8 inches (15.25 to 20.5 cm) apart along the circumference of the circle, but leave a gap of about 2 or 3 feet (61 to 91.5 m) on the north side of the teepee.

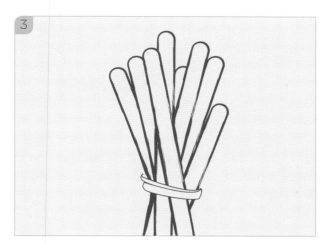

Step 3: Secure the tops of the poles with string or wire.

Step 4: Plant pole bean seeds at the base of each pole.

Tomato Supports

Considerable controversy exists among expert gardeners as to the best way to support tomatoes. The tomato is a tropical sprawler by nature, one that gardeners everywhere have tried to tame by various devices.

Among the most powerful tools in the tomato trellis arsenal is genetics: determinate tomatoes naturally remain smaller, stockier, and less likely to escape across the fence than the indeterminate types that are the majority of tomatoes. Determinate tomatoes are most easily supported with a wire cage about 18 inches (45.75 cm) in diameter and 4 to 6 feet (1.25 to 2 m) tall. Cages may be purchased ready-made, or fabricated from concrete reinforcing wire, livestock fencing, or a similar material. The openings in the cage must be large enough to permit easy access for rearranging the plant's stems and to harvest the fruit. To keep the whole arrangement from tipping in high wind, secure the cage to a sturdy stake driven at least 2 feet (.5 m) into the ground near the base of the plant. The stake should extend the full height of the cage for maximum stability.

You can also support determinate tomatoes with a single stake, 7 or 8 feet (2 to 2.5 m) in length, driven 2 feet (61 cm) into the ground. It is best to install the stake at transplanting time, to avoid damaging the roots of the tomato. When the plant is about 2 feet tall, tie it loosely to the stake with soft twine or strips of cloth, placing them just below the point where a leaf leaves the stem. Keep adding additional ties every foot or so as the plant grows. This method is more trouble than relying on a cage, but is hard to beat for simplicity, effectiveness, and low cost.

Indeterminate tomatoes, the majority of varieties, require a much larger cage or another type of support. They can be woven by hand into the network of a string trellis, as described previously. The stems can be tied individually to a series of stakes, interconnected with horizontal poles to afford stability. A quick internet search will turn up dozens of ways, from the simple to the bizarre, to support tomatoes. The best advice is to choose whatever support seems best for your circumstances, but realize that all tomatoes require sturdy support of the appropriate size.

It is worth noting that tomatoes will grow much larger where summers are warm and the growing season is long. In cooler climates, tomato supports need not be as large and extensive as those required elsewhere.

Galvanized livestock fencing was used to make this simple wire trellis.

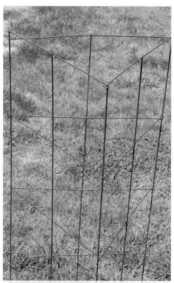

This type of wire tomato cage can be folded for storage.

Welded, galvanized tomato cages are available at garden centers.

Planting Transplants

Whether you start plants at home yourself or purchase them at a garden center, in order to keep them healthy and growing they must be correctly transplanted to their permanent spot in the garden. Young plants are often tender and easily damaged. In particular, getting the root system out of the container and into the ground without incident is necessary if the plant is to grow properly. With that cautionary note, handling transplants presents no serious challenges.

Step 1: Prepare the planting area and decide approximately where each plant will go before you begin. Keep in mind the recommended spacing for the specific variety you are planting.

Step 2: Water the cell tray of seedlings before you begin. Remove a seedling from the tray by gently pushing upward on the bottom of the cell with one hand, while simultaneously grasping the plant and gently pulling it from the cell.

Step 3: Dig a hole a little larger than the root mass, using a hand spade or your hands, and place the seedling in the hole. If recommended, add fertilizer to the hole before inserting the seedling.

Step 4: Firm the soil around the seedling. Make sure the crown of the seedling is sitting at the same level as it was in the cell tray.

Step 5: Side-dress the seedlings with fertilizer, if recommended.

Step 6: Water the bed thoroughly to settle the soil around the roots of the transplants and prevent them from wilting.

If the seedlings have remained too long in the cell tray, their roots may be matted at the bottom of the cell. In this case, after removing the seedling from the cell, use your thumb and forefinger to pinch the bottom of the root mass, twisting it free from the rest of the roots. Then proceed as directed above. Failing to trim crowded roots in this manner may result in stunted plants.

Direct Sowing Seed

Although it is recommended that beginning gardeners purchase transplants of many of the crops they will grow, some vegetables do best if their seeds are sown in the soil. Gardeners call this process *direct seeding,* and it could not be simpler.

Depending upon the crop, you will either sow seeds in rows or hills or scatter them over a wider area. The latter approach is known as *broadcasting* the seeds.

Broadcasting is often used for leafy green crops, either individually or in mixed sowings. Plants form a dense blanket of leaves that is then harvested with scissors, and the plants are left to resprout for another harvest, a technique known as *cut and come again.* Cover crops are also broadcast-seeded.

Radish seeds are sprinkled directly into a prepared furrow.

When the radish seeds sprout, they will be too close together and must be thinned.

Broadcasting is a useful method for producing your own transplants, provided the climate is suitable for sowing outdoors at the proper time. Vegetables such as spinach, corn salad, and kale can be started in a small patch, from which individual plants are removed and transferred to a permanent growing spot. Late tomato and pepper plants may also be started this way.

Planting in rows is helpful for crops that require early thinning. The two most common ones are radishes and carrots. A shallow furrow is made in the growing bed and seeds are scattered every 1 inch (2.5 cm) or so along its length. After germination occurs, plants are removed to allow those remaining to grow at the correct spacing. This approach is easier than making hills when the seeds are small. For large-seeded plants like squash, cucumbers, and legumes, the seeds can be planted in hills, with individual planting spots spaced at the correct distance for the crop. Typically, several seeds are planted at each location. After germination, all but one to three of the plants are allowed to remain to produce the crop.

Hill planting is also useful when vegetables are used in clumps. Scallions, bunching onions, and cilantro are examples of this type of crop. Several of the small seeds are planted in each hill, and at harvest time the entire clump is removed for the kitchen. This method avoids disturbing the other plants in the area when one clump is dug, leaving them to grow for a future harvest.

Use a pair of tweezers to thin small seedlings like lettuce while they are still in the seed tray.

Thinning

Of all the skills novice gardeners seem to avoid acquiring, thinning is number one. The reluctance to remove and destroy baby plants that you have just nurtured into germination and early growth is understandable. We humans are, after all, by nature compassionate toward the small and weak, even if we eventually plan to kill and eat them. But we must overcome this tendency and thin, thin, thin.

Thinning vegetable seedlings confers numerous advantages upon the lucky few that are left behind to prosper. Reducing the crowded seed bed to proper spacing allows individual plants a larger share of the available sunshine, water, and nutrients afforded by the site. In fact, studies have demonstrated that proper plant spacing results in a larger weight of harvest from fewer individual plants than is the case when plants are not thinned and many are allowed to grow together in the same space.

The seeming "losses" from thinning can often be turned into something useful, too. For example, small plants of beets, chard, spinach, and several others can be added to salads as baby greens.

Leeks and garlic can be planted at a closer-than-recommended spacing as a hedge against losses. After the plants have achieved about half their expected growth, every other one can be pulled. Such baby leeks and garlic command a premium price at the produce market. This method also works with storage onions. The smaller plants will have a milder, sweeter taste than their mature compatriots.

The timing of thinning can be crucial for some crops. For example, radishes should be thinned before their true leaves appear for maximum root development. Because they grow so quickly, this can mean thinning only a few days after germination. Carrots will never develop full-sized roots if not thinned before the tops are 3 inches (7.5 cm) tall. Beets need thinning as soon as the true leaves appear to produce the most uniform-sized roots.

Because carrots germinate more slowly than radishes, the two can be sown together in the same row. Radishes will germinate first, and are thinned as just explained. By the time the radishes are ready to harvest, roughly a month after sowing, the carrots will be at the proper size for thinning. Pulling the radishes automatically uproots some carrot seedlings and loosens the soil, making the job of hand thinning much easier.

Corn salad seedlings (foreground) have room to grow after transplanting from the germination container.

Proper spacing results in a better harvest.

Using Seed Tape

Much of the effort required to thin vegetables has been eliminated with the invention of seed tape. Available from certain seed suppliers, this is a biodegradable paper tape into which have been embedded the seeds of vegetables at a convenient spacing that requires only a minimal amount of thinning, if any, after the plants have germinated. Installing seed tape in the garden is simple and straightforward.

Step 1: Make a furrow in the soil, at the recommended depth for the vegetable variety being planted. Lay the free end of the seed tape at one end of the furrow. A small stone will hold it in place.

Step 2: Unroll the tape along the length of the furrow, and cut with scissors. Secure the end in place with a handful of soil.

Step 3: Cover the tape with soil to the correct depth for the vegetable variety. Water well.

Seed tape germination of beets at approximately the final spacing.

Seeds will germinate normally and break through the soft paper tape, arriving at the surface well separated from each other. Additional hand thinning may be needed, depending upon the vegetable variety. Consult the package directions for additional information. Now and then, the tape will have two seeds in one spot, a manufacturing defect. Simply remove the weaker appearing of the two seedlings.

One drawback to the use of seed tape is the limited number of varieties available. The most commonly available species are radishes, beets, carrots, lettuce, and spinach, and within these species only a limited number of cultivars may be offered. That being said, often seed tape is made with the most popular and easily grown cultivars, based upon the seed company's experience. The cultivars are a good bet for success for the novice backyard gardener, regardless of location.

Thin seedlings to their final spacing when true leaves appear.

Planting Bulbs and Tubers

Although the majority of vegetables are produced from seeds, a few are started from miniature versions of the mature plant. Notably, bulb-forming onion and potato "seeds" are of this type.

Onion Bulbs

Bulb-forming onions are started from sets—small bulbs about the size of a marble that are produced commercially. Certain perennial onions also produce sets (short for *offsets* from the main bulb) that are replanted to increase the size of the patch.

To grow onions from sets, the sets are simply pressed into well-prepared soil until only about half the little bulb appears above the soil line. Make sure to place them right side up, with the pointed tips aimed toward the sky. Leaving the upper portion of the bulb uncovered allows for its maximum expansion with less resistance from the soil when the plant is ready to mature its crop. After planting, the area should be watered thoroughly to settle the new plants into the soil and stimulate rapid root growth.

Some onions are grown from small bulbs called *sets*.

Onion sets are pressed about halfway into the soil.

These onions sprouted from sets placed about two weeks previously.

Potato seed tubers should have at least three sets of buds, or "eyes."

Potato Tubers

Seed potatoes, as they are called, are small tubers separated from the rest of the crop at harvest time and held in storage until the following spring. Most seed potatoes are produced in areas that are free of damaging viruses. The prevalence of viruses is one reason for the oft-seen recommendation to avoid planting potatoes from the grocery store, despite the fact that they will often sprout normally and grow a crop of potatoes. Once a given virus has contaminated your growing area, science offers no method of control, apart from avoiding that crop for a few years. Therefore, if you plan on growing potatoes on a regular basis, always purchase certified virus-free seed stock.

Each small potato has several "eyes" or growth buds, from which new potato plants will develop. If the seed potato is large, it can be cut into smaller pieces for sowing. Each piece should be larger than a golf ball, and should have at least three eyes. After cutting, some gardeners dust the cut surface with powdered sulfur to prevent rot. The pieces can also be allowed to dry out on newspaper for a few days before planting. If the seed tubers are smaller than about 2 inches (5 cm) in diameter, you will get better results from just planting the whole thing.

Potato tubers should be planted about 4 inches (10 cm) below the soil surface. The entire potato crop will form between the tuber and the soil surface. Therefore, potatoes are "hilled up" by adding additional soil as they grow. See the section devoted to potatoes for additional information.

Intercropping

Intercropping is the practice of planting two compatible vegetable or herb varieties in a shared space. This allows a limited growing area to do double duty for crop production.

Compatible Varieties

In order for intercropping to be successful, the two vegetable varieties must be compatible. Their growth requirements must be approximately equal, and the development of one should not interfere with the development of the other.

Often one crop of the pair is a fast-maturing variety that is harvested long before the other reaches maturity. A good example of this companionship is arugula and cabbage. The arugula is seeded first by broadcasting over the planting area. As soon as arugula seedlings emerge, the cabbage plants are installed in the bed. (Never mind the destruction of a few seedlings in the process; the rest will make up for the loss with added productivity.)

Other good combinations for intercropping are lettuce with onions, carrots with peas, and beans with corn. In the latter case, the beans climb the cornstalks, eliminating the need for installing poles.

Planting Tables

The following tables provide multiple examples of good and poor vegetable and herb companions. For simplicity, the word *brassicas* is used to refer to all members of the cabbage family.

Vegetable Companions

Crop	Good Companion
bean	brassicas, carrot, cucumber, eggplant, pea, potato, Swiss chard
beet	bean, brassicas, garlic, lettuce, onion
brassicas	beet, cucumber, garlic, lettuce, onion, potato, spinach, Swiss chard
carrot	bean, lettuce, onion, pea, pepper, tomato
cucumber	bean, brassicas, lettuce, tomato
eggplant	bean, pepper
lettuce	beet, brassicas, carrot, garlic, onion
melon	pumpkin, squash
onion	beet, brassicas, carrot, lettuce, pepper, Swiss chard, tomato
pea	bean, carrot, cucumber, turnip
pepper	carrot, eggplant, onion, tomato
potato	bean, brassicas, eggplant, pea
spinach	brassicas
squash	melon
tomato	asparagus, bean, carrot, cucumber, onion, pepper, turnip, pea

Herb and Edible Flower Companions

Herb/Flower	Vegetable Companions
basil	pepper, tomato
bee balm	tomato
borage	bean, squash, tomato
calendula	asparagus, tomato
chive	carrot, lettuce, tomato
dill	brassicas, lettuce, onion
garlic	beet, brassicas, lettuce
lovage	bean
marigold	bean, cucumber, eggplant, melon, potato, squash
mint	brassicas, tomato
oregano	bean
parsley	asparagus, tomato
rosemary	bean, brassicas
sage	brassicas, carrot, tomato
thyme	brassicas, carrot, eggplant, tomato

Poor Companions

Because they compete with each other or attract the same pests, some plants are poor companions.

Vegetable	Avoid Planting Near
bean	chive, garlic, leek, onion, shallot
beet	pole bean
brassicas	other brassicas, nasturtium, pole bean, tomato
carrot	dill

Vegetable	Avoid Planting Near
cucumber	potato, sage
pea	chive, garlic, leek, onion, shallot
potato	cucumber, squash, tomato
sweet potato	most other vegetable crops
tomato	dill, brassicas, potato

Irrigation

In an ideal world, rainfall would supply all the water your garden needs. When natural rainfall is not enough, however, or the weather is unexpectedly hot and dry, you will need to supply extra water to bring in a successful crop. As has been repeatedly mentioned throughout the book, vegetables need at least 1 inch (2.5 cm) of water per week. This is about 65 gallons (227 L) per 100 square feet (30.5 m) of growing space.

Watering Can

The simplest irrigation method is to carry water to the plants in a watering can. You might find a good one at a yard sale or junk shop. Garden centers sell them in all sizes.

Garden Hose

A good garden hose is the choice of most backyard gardeners for irrigation. It must be long enough to reach all the places you might need to water. Better-quality hoses can last a lifetime and are a good investment. Look for heavy brass fittings, reinforced tubing, and a no-kink guarantee. Hose attachments and fittings should be solid brass. They cost more but will outlast plastic or soft metal products.

Watering by hand with a hose helps conserve water. You can apply water directly to the plant's roots, and avoid wetting foliage, which can encourage disease.

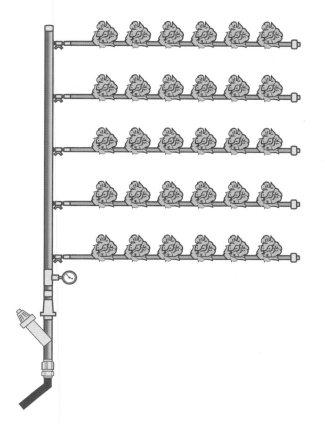

Drip Irrigation

One of the most water-conserving methods is drip irrigation. In a typical system, the water tap is connected to a header hose. From the header hose, smaller emitter hoses deliver water at the base of each plant in the row. Drip tape, a flattened hose with tiny openings for water to ooze out, is also used. It will release a continuous band of water along the row of plants.

Water pressure is controlled by a regulator, to achieve just the right drip rate automatically. A hose timer can also be used to control the amount of irrigation supplied. In some locations, a filter should be installed at the point where water enters the header hose to remove fine debris that might eventually clog emitters or drip tape.

Drip irrigation systems can be adapted for beds, containers, or in-ground rows, but the larger the growing area, the greater the initial investment in equipment. Indoor growing spaces seem ideal spots for this type of system because splashes and splatters are minimized. Only you can decide whether this makes sense in your situation.

Overhead Irrigation

Overhead spray irrigation equipment wastes a lot of water and should be avoided where possible.

Mulch

Mulch is any material applied around growing plants to cover the soil. Mulch can be organic in nature and left to decompose and enrich the planting bed. For some special purposes, mulch can be a synthetic material, such as black plastic film.

Benefits of Mulch

Mulch provides numerous benefits. Chief among these is slowing the rate of evaporation and thus keeping soil evenly moist, a prime consideration for vegetable production. When applied at the proper time, mulch can help keep soil either cool or warm, depending upon the gardener's purposes. Mulch prevents soil-borne microorganisms from reaching plant leaves, by preventing splashing of soil when the bed is irrigated. Mulch also provides a habitat for beneficial insects and spiders that prey on plant pests.

Mulch Materials

Mulch can be any material you may have available. Pine needles, shredded hardwood bark, wood chips, compost, straw, and even shredded office paper can be used as mulch. The only requirement is that the material be loose, fluffy, and nontoxic. In a pinch, even sheets of newspaper or thin cardboard can be cut and placed around plants to achieve an effective, if somewhat unsightly, mulch.

Using black plastic mulch warms the soil.

These leeks have been mulched with pine needles.

The most commonly used synthetic mulch is plastic film. Different types are employed for different purposes. Black plastic film is frequently used as mulch for heat-loving crops like melons. The growing bed is first covered with a layer of the plastic. The plastic is slit in places and seeds or plants are planted beneath the slits. Using black plastic mulch makes possible the production of heat-requiring plants in cooler-climate areas.

Clear plastic mulch can be used to "sterilize" a growing area that has seen disease or weed problems. Placed over the soil surface and held tightly in place, the clear plastic traps heat underneath in the same way that the glazing of a greenhouse does. Temperatures beneath the plastic can reach levels sufficient to kill soil-borne pathogens and weed seeds.

In recent years, red plastic mulch has been employed in the production of fruit crops, tomatoes being the prime example. Research has demonstrated that the red light reflected up from the mulch increases fruit production.

Timing of Mulch Installation

Regardless of the type of mulch you choose, it must be applied at the proper time for the crop you are growing. A classic mistake is to mulch warm-season crops too soon after planting. For these vegetables, wait until the soil has thoroughly warmed up before applying mulch, or the soil may remain too cool for optimal plant growth.

Fertilizers

Commercially prepared fertilizer products are labeled with the percentages by weight of nitrogen, phosphorus, and potassium they contain. A cost comparison between any two fertilizer products is easy to calculate. Just figure how much the nitrogen in each product costs per pound. Because nitrogen is often the limiting factor for plant growth, and because phosphorus and potassium are relatively abundant and cheap, the nitrogen component is the cost factor in all fertilizers.

The label tells you 1) the percentage by weight of nitrogen and 2) the total weight of the bag.

Therefore, in a 5-pound (2.25 kg) bag of 10-10-10 fertilizer, $\frac{1}{2}$ pound (226.8 g) (10 percent of 5 pounds) is nitrogen. If the bag costs $8.00, the cost per pound of nitrogen is $16.00. (8/0.5 = 16)

Carry out the same calculation on a second product, and it is easy to compare the price.

As a general rule, for vegetable production a "balanced" fertilizer is recommended. This means the three primary components, N-P-K, are present in equal or approximately equal amounts. A product labeled 10-10-10 or 8-7-8 would be considered balanced, while 20-10-5 would not be balanced. The latter product is a high-nitrogen fertilizer. This product would be suitable for plants with big demands for nitrogen, such as corn or spinach.

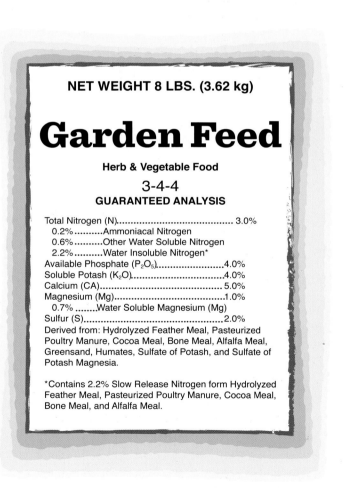

NET WEIGHT 8 LBS. (3.62 kg)

Garden Feed

Herb & Vegetable Food

3-4-4
GUARANTEED ANALYSIS

Total Nitrogen (N)...3.0%
   0.2% ....Ammoniacal Nitrogen
   0.6% ....Other Water Soluble Nitrogen
   2.2% ....Water Insoluble Nitrogen*
Available Phosphate (P_2O_5).........................4.0%
Soluble Potash (K_2O)..................................4.0%
Calcium (CA)...5.0%
Magnesium (Mg)..1.0%
   0.7% ....Water Soluble Magnesium (Mg)
Sulfur (S)..2.0%
Derived from: Hydrolyzed Feather Meal, Pasteurized Poultry Manure, Cocoa Meal, Bone Meal, Alfalfa Meal, Greensand, Humates, Sulfate of Potash, and Sulfate of Potash Magnesia.

*Contains 2.2% Slow Release Nitrogen form Hydrolyzed Feather Meal, Pasteurized Poultry Manure, Cocoa Meal, Bone Meal, and Alfalfa Meal.

Cottonseed meal is one of several possible sources of organic nitrogen.

Bone meal is a great organic phosphorus source.

Balanced organic fertilizer products are available commercially, or you may want to go the less expensive route of purchasing components separately and using them at your discretion.

Nitrogen Sources:

- Cottonseed meal
- Alfalfa meal
- Blood meal
- Kelp granules

Phosphorus Sources:

- Bone Meal
- Powdered Phosphate Rock
- Super-phosphate (acid-treated phosphate rock)

Potassium Sources:

- Greensand
- Wood Ashes

You may find it helpful to keep one or more of these products on hand for use in your vegetable garden. For example, *side dressing,* or adding fertilizer to the soil adjacent to growing plants, is a great way to renew a bed of greens after they have been cut. You would use a nitrogen source for this purpose. Similarly, for a planting of fall beets or carrots following a summer planting of corn, you might add both alfalfa meal and phosphate rock to improve the soil fertility before planting the root vegetables. Being able to target specific plant nutrition needs is the main benefit of this approach. You also avoid wasting a more expensive, balanced product when some of its nutrients are already present in the soil.

Liquid Fertilizers

When plant nutrients are supplied in soluble form, already dissolved in water, they are immediately available for uptake by growing plants. This makes liquid preparations especially useful when you desire to stimulate production after harvest, as with greens that are cut and then permitted to regrow.

Liquid fertilizer can be applied to plants with a watering can, or you can purchase a siphon attachment and plastic tubing that permits adding fertilizer solution from a bucket as you irrigate the garden with a hose. This method is suitable for larger gardens, where repeated trips with the watering can would prove laborious.

Two good liquid fertilizers that are commercially available are fish emulsion and seaweed extract. These are usually supplied in concentrates that must be diluted before use. Follow label directions for dilution.

You can also prepare a fertilizer "tea" using materials available at home. The method is a simple one. It works just like making tea from tea leaves, but you extract the water-soluble nutrients from a nutrient-rich material. Good candidates are well-rotted manure from cattle, sheep, poultry, rabbits, horses, or goats. (Never use the manure from carnivorous animals, like dogs and cats.) Other possibilities are prepared compost, and certain plants that decompose quickly.

This brass siphon attaches to a garden hose and permits adding liquid fertilizer to irrigation water.

Step 1: Place a shovelful of manure or your chosen compost material in a 5-gallon (8.9 L) plastic bucket, and fill with water.

Step 2: Let the bucket sit for a couple of days. Stir the mixture a few times each day to release more nutrients into the water.

Step 3: Carefully decant the tea from the bucket into a watering can and apply to the growing area. Use the finished tea within 24 hours, or bacteria will utilize the extracted nutrients.

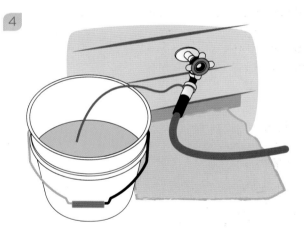

Step 4: Connect one end of a plastic tube to a siphon attached to the garden hose, and place the other end in the bucket. This allows the tea to mix with water as you irrigate.

Comfrey (*Symphytum officinale*) makes a nutrient-rich fertilizer tea. The leaves can be repeatedly harvested from a single planting. Mixed with water in a bucket, they quickly break down to yield a liquid fertilizer solution. Fresh, green grass clippings will also react this way, although the bucket will smell somewhat like fresh cow manure. Alfalfa hay, cottonseed meal, and shredded leaves will all produce teas with varying levels of plant nutrients. Experiment with whatever material you have available in sufficient quantity.

Cover Crops

Cover-cropping merely involves following up a harvested crop with a planting designed to restore soil fertility. Cover crops are sometimes called *green manure* because they are incorporated into the soil rather than being harvested. For example, after closing down a growing bed, you could plant winter ryegrass. This annual grass grows quickly and tolerates winter cold. In early spring, the grass is tilled under to enrich the soil for a crop of vegetables.

Legumes such as clover are frequently used as cover crops because of the nitrogen-fixing bacteria associated with legume roots. Clover, vetch, alfalfa, and field peas are among the commonly used legume cover crops.

Besides providing nutrients when they are tilled under, while growing the cover crop shades out weed seedlings, leaving fewer weeding chores when the space is planted later with vegetable crops.

Deep-rooted cover crops can actually absorb minerals such as calcium from deeper soil layers. When the cover crop eventually decomposes, these minerals become available in the surface soil.

In addition to annual grasses and legumes, other cover crops include buckwheat, which is good for warm-season cover, and oats, which thrives in cooler weather.

Regardless of the cover crop chosen, it will require some maintenance in order to achieve lush growth before it is time to incorporate it into the soil. Watering will be needed if rainfall is insufficient for the cover crop. Grasses typically mature with less water than broad-leaved crops, and should be selected if the cover cropping season is expected to be dry.

The best time to kill the cover crop is just as its blooms appear. The individual plants will contain the maximum amount of nutrients at that time. Cut down the cover crop at the soil line, allow it to wilt on the soil for a few days, and till or spade it into the bed.

Incorporating the cover crop should be done approximately 30 days before you intend to replant to allow sufficient time for decomposition to begin releasing nutrients into the soil.

Clover and other legumes
often top the list of preferred
cover crops.

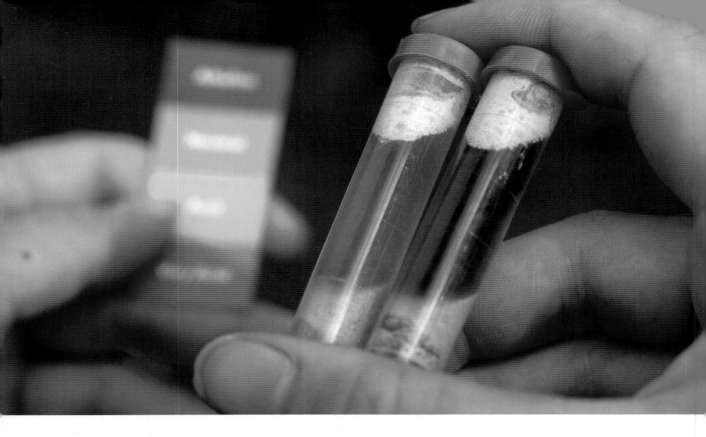

Soil Testing

Whether you use in-ground or raised beds for your food garden, it is wise to test the soil periodically. This avoids guesswork when applying amendments to adjust the pH of the soil or to improve fertility.

Soil Testing Services

The most accurate and exhaustive soil analysis will be obtained from a professional service. Along with the test results, you will receive a list of recommendations as to the types and amounts of amendments needed for vegetable production. This kind of information is extremely helpful, but you must pay a fee to obtain it. For most backyard growers, a do-it-yourself test kit offers the best option.

Do-It-Yourself Kits

As the accompanying illustrations demonstrate, soil test kits are not all that different from kits used to test swimming pools. Kits typically have four tests: pH, nitrate, phosphorus, and potassium. Using any kit is simple and straightforward, but for best results read and carefully follow the instructions provided by the manufacturer. In general, you will:

1. Collect a soil sample. Scoop up a small amount of soil from each of several spots in your growing area. Mix these together thoroughly in a clean container. Then remove the required amount of soil for each test. This will provide results that reflect average conditions across the entire growing space.

2. Mix the soil with water and add test chemicals, carefully following the manufacturer's instructions.

3. Compare the color of the sample to the color chart or scale supplied with the kit to determine the resulting values.

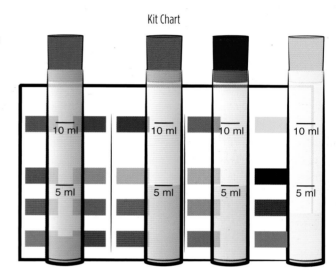

Kit Chart

The literature supplied with the kit will typically offer general recommendations for improving soil conditions in cases where the results indicate that action is needed.

Take care to dispose of test samples properly. Wash your hands after working with the test chemicals, and keep all such products out of children's reach.

What to Expect from a Testing Service

In the United States, the USDA operates agriculture extension offices across the country. All offer soil testing services. Locate one nearest you online at www.csrees.usda.gov/Extension/. Private testing laboratories also offer soil testing in many locations.

The service, whether government or private, will usually provide a sample container, which is mailed to you along with instructions for taking the sample. You then ship the container back to the laboratory. Within a short time, you will receive a report of the analysis and recommendations for amendments, if any.

Weeds

Weeds growing in your garden can reduce yield by more than half. Weeds compete with your vegetables for sunshine, water, and fertilizer, and can even release chemicals that inhibit other plants growing near them. Different areas of the world will have different types of weeds, depending upon climate and soil types. Learn to recognize the common weeds that appear in your garden and take steps to minimize their impact.

Perennial Weeds

Perennial weeds are the most pernicious, because if left unmolested they will return year after year, healthier and more vigorous each time. They also will produce thousands of seeds to spread themselves throughout your garden. Perennial weeds must be dug out root and all or they will sprout right back. Dig them out as soon as you notice them.

Weeds with a sturdy rootstock will return unless uprooted completely.

Annual Weeds

The key to controlling annual weeds lies in preventing the current crop from making seeds for a future crop. Annual weeds may be pulled by hand, killed by shallow cultivation, or smothered with an organic mulch.

Some annual weed seeds are capable of lying dormant in the soil for years. When the area is cultivated, they respond to even minimal exposure to sunlight by germinating. Therefore, a second round of cultivation becomes necessary to destroy the young sprouts. That in turn may expose additional seeds, creating a vicious cycle. Mulching instead of cultivating shuts out the light and breaks the cycle.

Annual weeds in open beds may also be controlled by means of a germination inhibitor. A commonly used organic one is wheat gluten, available in a variety of commercial preparations. As a rule, a certain period of time must elapse before the treated area can be used for sowing vegetable seeds, although the inhibitor has no effect on growing plants, such as tomato transplants.

Pernicious Pest Plants

Some weeds are so invasive and tenacious that a large patch of them may require professional assistance and possibly the application of chemical herbicide to control. As long as this is done with proper attention to dosage rates and timing, the soil can recover. After the weeds are dead, the soil can be amended with compost or other organic materials, covered with a heavy mulch and allowed to lie fallow for a year before using it for growing vegetables.

One of the benefits of growing in raised beds is that weeds become less of a problem over time. The only weeds that appear are from seeds blown in by the wind.

Weeds compete with vegetables for water and fertilizer and should be removed promptly.

Basic Pest Control

Proper culture practices will go a long way toward preventing problems with garden pests and disease. Vegetables are somewhat like pedigreed dogs: they need more attention and coddling than many other types of plants. When vegetables are stressed by insufficient moisture, not enough sun, or the lack of a crucial nutrient, they respond with chemical signals that insects have evolved to seek out.

While it is not possible to summarize the methods for controlling every possible insect pest, several basic principles, if kept in mind, will arm you to deal with the most common ones.

Guidelines for Controlling Insects

1. Follow all recommendations for cultivation of the crops you select.

2. Inspect your garden frequently, so you can identify insect problems when they are in the early stages. Insects often hide on the undersides of leaves. Turn over a few leaves here and there to look for infestations.

3. Insect eggs that you may find attached to your plants invariably hatch into something that will feed on the plant. Destroy all egg clusters that you find.

4. Aphids are found everywhere and are often the first insects to arrive on stressed plants. They feed by sucking plant juices and multiply rapidly. In the early stages of infestation, simply washing them off with a jet of water from the hose can be an effective remedy.

5. Insects that chew holes in leaves or stems will respond to organic pesticides that must be ingested to be effective. Sucking insects, on the other hand, obtain food from inside the plant, and are not susceptible to ingestion pesticides. Rather, they must be attacked with contact pesticides.

6. Some types of vegetable pests are seasonal in a given region, and can be thwarted by timing plantings to coincide with the time that the insect population is lowest.

7. Plants grown under any type of plastic covering are more susceptible to insect attack than plants covered with "breathable" materials. Besides trapping heat, plastic increases humidity and lowers air circulation, creating ideal conditions for some types of insects to flourish. Always remove plant covers at the earliest practical time.

Cabbage worms are a major pest of this family of crops.

Cucumber beetles and other insect pests are best combatted by proper plant husbandry.

The tomato hornworm caterpillar can devastate a plant in a single day.

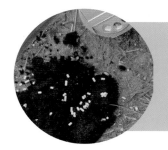

Placing slug bait on coffee grounds enhances its effectiveness.

Disease Prevention

Although treatment is sometimes possible, diseased vegetable crops are often best removed from the garden to prevent the disease from spreading. As with insect attacks, disease strikes plants that are stressed, usually from improper cultural practices.

It is not possible to address every possible plant disease, but general guidelines can be given that will enable you to control most types of disease problems.

Bacterial Disease

We often think of bacteria in terms of disease production, but in the garden the vast majority of bacteria are beneficial. When bacterial disease does strike vegetable plants, the result is often the rapid decline and death of the plant. Excessively soggy soil frequently results in bacterial root rot. Roots drown from lack of oxygen and begin to die, and bacteria invade easily.

Water standing in the crowns of some plants may also allow rot to develop.

Few effective cures exist for bacterial disease. Provide proper drainage and avoid wetting foliage, and bacterial problems will be far less likely.

Keeping the garden free of dead plant debris removes a potential source of disease organisms.

Fungal diseases, such as this powdery mildew, are often brought on by warm, overly wet conditions or poor air circulation.

Fungal Disease

Numerous vegetable diseases are caused by fungi, whose tiny spores are carried by the wind throughout the world. Treatments exist for controlling certain types of fungi, but the best precaution the gardener can take is to grow genetically resistant varieties. The information on disease resistance for specific cultivars will be found in seed catalog listings. There are also a few basic precautions gardeners can take to prevent disease from taking hold.

Fungi are often transferred from the soil to the plant by water splashing on the leaves. Apply a mulch around the base of the plants, and avoid directing water on the plants from above. Instead, water the soil.

Warm, humid conditions with little air movement allow fungi to grow rapidly. Especially for warm-weather crops, proper spacing between plants is essential to allow for good air circulation. If the chance for heat stress exists, as in areas where temperatures exceed 90°F, extra space should be allotted between individual plants.

One seemingly universal fungus is powdery mildew, which gives the leaves the appearance of having been sprinkled with fine gray dust. Heat and water stress may cause cucumbers, squash, and melons to develop this problem. Cool, damp, and cloudy conditions contribute to the proliferation of mildew on greens like spinach. If the cool season is often overcast, gardeners should give spinach and other leafy greens wider than recommended spacing.

Crop Rotation: Why?

Different vegetables remove different amounts of nutrients from the soil. Similarly, pests and diseases that affect one vegetable may not affect others. The best method to avoid wearing out your soil and encouraging disease is crop rotation. The easiest way to manage crop rotation is to group vegetables together. A given bed should not be planted with vegetables from the same group in two successive seasons. Ideally, you would plant vegetables from the same group in the same spot only once in every four or five years.

The crop rotation groups and their members are:

Leaves, Stems, or Flowers

arugula, Belgian endive, broccoli, Brussels sprouts, cabbage, cauliflower, chervil, cilantro, celery, celery root, collards, corn, curly endive, escarole, kale, kohlrabi, mustard, lettuces, okra, parsley, radicchio, spinach, Swiss chard, upland cress, watercress

Fruits

cucumber, eggplant, pepper, potato, strawberry, summer squash, winter squash, tomatillo, tomato

Root Crops

beet, carrot, onion, leek, potato, radish, rutabaga, sweet potato, turnip,

Legumes

bean, pea, soybean, cover crop

Plants from different rotation groups can often be interplanted with each other, depending upon other factors. Some good combinations are lettuce and scallions, peas and carrots, and corn and beans.

Even the smallest garden can benefit from rotation. If you don't have many individual planting beds, subdivide your existing beds into "rotation zones" and keep track of what is planted where each season.

Potatoes, tomatoes, and strawberries are subject to many of the same diseases, and should not follow each other in the same location.

Legumes add nitrogen to the soil, owing to the actions of beneficial bacteria living on their roots. Along with cover crops, peas and beans can help to rebuild soil nutrients depleted by one of the other groups. Keeping this aspect of rotation in mind is essential for long-term soil health.

Follow root crops with legumes because the former break up the soil, and the latter like loosely textured soils.

Beans, leeks, and cilantro (rear) belong to different rotation groups.

Crop Rotation: How?

The accompanying illustrations provide a visual guide to crop rotation using four planting beds. It is not necessary to follow this pattern exactly. Some vegetables, in some locations, are seldom troubled by disease and can be planted as you wish. Carrots, turnips, and beans often number among the least troublesome plants in the garden, for example.

Nevertheless, it is always better to avoid planting the same crop in the same spot year after year. Different types of crops make differing demands upon the soil. For example, corn requires a lot of nitrogen, but beets need more phosphorus and less nitrogen. When the same crop grows in the same place year after year, the nutrients most important to that crop become depleted. Often, this results in each successive crop being less productive than the preceding one.

Within the various plant groups, avoid planting the same varieties over and over, also. Variations in disease resistance or other factors may be problematic when the same cultivar is always used. Heirloom tomatoes may have very little disease resistance, while modern hybrids enjoy resistance to multiple diseases. Following up a hybrid with an heirloom in the same soil invites disease in the heirloom.

Bear in mind that crop rotation is not a substitute for building soil via the addition of compost and fertilizers. Nutrients depleted by the previous crop do not magically reappear when another crop grows in the same spot. Following each harvest with an application of balanced organic fertilizer will help maintain soil fertility. Adding compost, as a mulch or when beds are prepared in spring, adds beneficial microorganisms that compete with crop pathogens and help maintain healthy conditions.

If a certain crop you want does not fit into the rotation schedule easily, grow it in a container instead. Container growers need not worry too much about rotation as they have the ability to discard the growing medium and start again with fresh, sterile medium should disease problems develop.

	Area 1	Area 2	Area 3	Area 4
Year 1	Leaves	Fruits	Roots	Legumes
Year 2	Fruits	Roots	Legumes	Leaves
Year 3	Roots	Legumes	Leaves	Fruits
Year 4	Legumes	Leaves	Fruits	Roots

Culture Problems

Some apparent plant diseases are actually due to improper cultural practices or deficiencies in soil chemistry. Besides the major elements—nitrogen, phosphorus, and potassium—plants require minor and trace elements for proper growth and development. When for some reason the plant is denied an essential element, symptoms become evident. Beginning gardeners often mistake these problems for disease.

While it is impossible to include all possible types of culture-related plant problems, we can describe the most common ones and suggest appropriate remedies.

Blossom End Rot

Blossom end rot occurs most commonly on tomatoes, but can also affect squash, peppers, and eggplant to a lesser degree. Two sets of circumstances can lead to the problem, which results when the plant is unable to obtain sufficient calcium from the soil. In the first case, the soil can be deficient in calcium. This may be the case in areas where native soil is acidic, or when acidic materials are used in growing media. Ground limestone applied to the planting area, at the rate of about a tablespoon per 10 square feet (3 square meters), will supply sufficient calcium.

The other way plants can be starved for calcium is uneven watering. Periods of abundant water alternating with drought as fruits are forming will encourage blossom end rot. In this situation, the water stress interferes with the plant's ability to absorb calcium from the soil. Thus, even though abundant calcium is present, blossom end rot still occurs.

Avoiding this problem can easily be accomplished by using mulch and paying attention to soil moisture levels on a regular basis, especially as fruit production gets underway.

Sunscald

Sunscald also affects tomatoes and peppers, and can be a problem for cool-season crops growing during warm weather. In the case of tomatoes and peppers, some varieties produce little foliage in relation to the amount of fruit set. Fruit that would normally be shaded by the plant's leaves is instead exposed to full sun. Fruits already damaged must be discarded, but the remedy for the rest of the crop is to provide shade during the hottest part of the day.

Tip Burn

If just the tips of a plant's leaves are turning brown, the plant is unable to transpire water at a sufficient rate for the ambient temperature. As a result, the outermost parts of the plant wilt, die, and turn brown. This is a frequent occurrence when cool-season plants are grown too warm, or if an unexpected warm spell arrives in early spring. Be prepared to increase irrigation during such events. If leaf tips are burning, even though the soil moisture is adequate, harvest what is usable and clear out the rest, replacing it with a different crop.

Trace Element Deficiencies

Weird, deformed plants, unusual hollow stalks, or other severe malformations may be due to viruses, but are more commonly associated with a trace element deficiency. Such problems are rare outside of commercial agriculture, but if you suspect you have an issue, professional help should be sought.

Vegetable Storage

Harvesting a bumper crop is less rewarding if you cannot store the harvest properly until it can be eaten. Different storage methods and conditions are suitable for different types of vegetables. Here are some examples of the most widely used methods and the vegetables to which they apply.

Plastic Bags and Boxes

Airtight plastic containers can be used for storing most vegetables and herbs that require refrigeration under what is often referred to as *root-cellar conditions*. Although a root cellar can be useful, most people rely on modern electric refrigeration. Moisture can be an issue for leafy greens and herbs, along with squash and cucumbers. Store these vegetables in perforated plastic bags that allow air to circulate. If you must use an airtight container, line it with paper towels to absorb excess moisture.

Prior to storage, wash vegetables in cold tap water and dry gently. Leafy greens can be dried by spinning in a kitchen device made for the purpose and will keep much longer if dry. Expect most vegetables to retain quality for a week with this type of storage.

Root Cellar or Crisper

Some vegetables retain quality for a long time if stored under cold, damp conditions. Many of these are root crops. Cabbage, carrots, beets, leeks, and celery all keep well with high humidity. A root cellar is simply an underground storage area that provides such conditions. Root cellars work best where winter is long and reliably cold without warm spells. Crops stored in layers of sand in a root cellar may keep well for months. Refrigerators are provided with a crisper that mimics root cellar conditions and is a suitable way to store small quantities.

Dry Storage

Certain vegetables store best in warm, dry conditions. Garlic, shallots, bulb onions, winter squash, and pumpkins all belong in this category.

Other vegetables, notably potatoes and sweet potatoes, should be stored cool and dry, but not at refrigeration temperatures. Both of these also need to be shielded from light, or they may be encouraged to sprout.

Countertop Storage

A few vegetables keep best when maintained at room temperature. Tomatoes, in particular, should never be exposed to temperatures below about 58°F to avoid loss of both flavor and texture. Some tomatoes and peppers have been bred to store very well at normal room temperature and humidity. Individual fruits should be wrapped in newspaper to protect adjacent fruit should one go bad.

Vegetable Preservation

Home gardeners have multiple options for long-term vegetable storage, usually described as *preservation*. The most commonly used methods are drying, freezing, canning, and pickling.

Drying Vegetables

In warm, arid regions, vegetables can often be dried simply by hanging them in a warm, breezy spot. This approach will be less successful where the climate is cool, humid, or both, in which case an electric dehydrator or kitchen range can be used to dry a wide range of crops. Among the most frequent candidates for drying are leafy herbs, hot peppers, green beans, and the seeds of legumes. Many other vegetables, including onions, shallots, leeks, carrots, and tomatoes, can be preserved by drying.

Dried vegetables should be transferred to clean, airtight containers and stored in the dark after the drying process is complete. Check home-dried vegetables regularly for the appearance of mold, which indicates too much moisture remained in the food. A small packet of silica gel, such as is often packaged with electronic equipment, can be placed in the storage container to help keep humidity at minimum.

Freezing

The freezer compartment of your refrigerator may be the very best place to preserve the flavor and nutritional value of homegrown produce. For successful home freezing, some vegetables must first be *blanched*. This involves dropping the prepared vegetables into boiling water for a short time (the duration of which depends upon the type of vegetable) and then draining them and plunging into cold water to stop the cooking process. Blanching not only sets the color of the vegetable, but also destroys enzymes that would slowly lead to flavor changes during storage. After blanching, the vegetables are placed in suitable containers, labeled, and moved to the freezer.

A few vegetables do not require blanching and can simply be prepared for cooking (peeled, cut into pieces, etc., as appropriate), dropped into freezer containers, and frozen. These include okra, peppers both sweet and hot, lemongrass, and ginger. Specific recommendations for individual vegetables can be found in cookbooks or online.

Canning

Home canning is enjoying a return to popularity. Among the favorite vegetables to can are tomatoes, green beans, potatoes, and corn. Home canning requires the proper equipment and strict attention to approved methods to avoid the possibility of deadly food-borne illnesses. Consult references before attempting to can your produce.

Pickling

Many vegetables can be pickled, which involves covering them with a solution that may contain varying amounts of salt, vinegar, and sugar, at concentrations sufficient to inhibit bacterial activity and prevent decomposition. Thousands of pickle recipes can be found in references, and their specifics should be adhered to for best results.

Your Garden Journal

Gardening is an acquired skill, and expertise is typically only gained after several seasons of experience. One of the best ways to develop expertise quickly is to keep track of what you did, when you did it, and what the results were. In other words, keep a journal and learn from your mistakes.

Whether your garden journal is committed to paper or digital bits, it should contain enough information about the garden to allow you to make informed decisions for the subsequent season.

At minimum, your journal should include:

- A list of vegetable varieties planted, and their location and planting date
- The date and amount of vegetables harvested from each planting
- The date and amount of any application of fertilizer or pesticide
- Comments on the weather, general appearance of the plants, and other information you deem significant

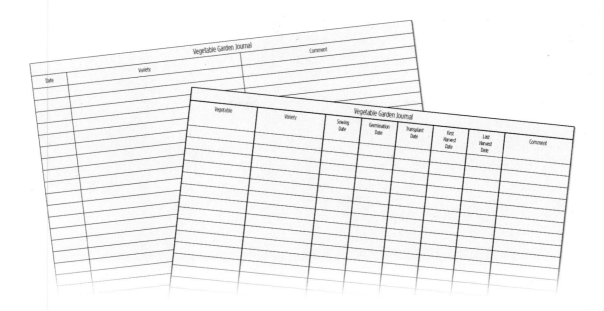

You may find it helpful to divide your journal into sections. You might have one section showing the layout of each growing bed with vegetable placement—a copy of the garden plan you made previously, in other words. A separate section, organized by the name of the vegetable, would compile seeding date, germination date, transplanting date, and date of first and last harvest. Because the same vegetable variety will perform differently under different conditions, keeping track of how that variety performs in your specific circumstances is your best guide to its future performance.

Some gardeners have a three-year rule: if you try the same vegetable variety for three years in a row and it does not perform to expectations, chances are it is not the gardener but the vegetable that is a failure. Try something else instead. There are many varieties to select from for the majority of vegetable species.

Go Digital

Some people never lose their appreciation for an old-fashioned paper and pencil journal. Nevertheless, using digital methods makes possible not only the storage of massive amounts of information, but also the rapid retrieval of just the information one is looking for when needed. Therefore, serious vegetable gardeners will use their computer to get the most out of their garden.

You can create your own gardening database using spreadsheet and word processing software, but there are numerous gardening software products available for every type of device. Phone and tablet apps are particularly useful, as they allow for data entry while the gardener is actually in the garden, rather than at a desk. Companies with an interest in attracting gardeners to their products now offer cloud-based applications that combine large information databases with a gardener-friendly interface.

Beyond the Basics

The information presented in the previous section should enable the average adult to build, plant, and maintain a reasonably productive vegetable garden on the first try. We have covered the basics of locating and planning the garden, sowing seed, and putting in transplants, and examined the main techniques for irrigating, controlling pests and diseases, and producing the most food from the available space by going vertical.

In this section, we will cover some additional techniques for the gardener who wants to go further. Considerable space, for example, is devoted to the preparation of compost and construction of a compost pile or bin. Converting garden and food wastes into compost that is, in turn, used to promote the production of food is the ultimate in recycling in the eyes of many. Composting at home does, however, require some attention to avoid creating odors or attracting vermin.

We have repeatedly recommended that beginning gardeners purchase started plants from a nursery for those vegetables that are not sown directly in the garden. In this section, we explain how to start your own transplants from seed or cuttings, saving on the cost of gardening and expanding the list of varieties you can grow.

Several pages are devoted to aspects of integrated pest management. Assuming you consider starting a home food garden a long-term project, integrated pest management offers techniques for progressively reducing the impact of pests on the garden without the use of chemical toxins.

The final pages of this section are concerned with extending the growing season beyond the norm for your area, whether by protecting plants growing outdoors with various devices, or by moving the food garden project indoors for the cold season.

Going beyond the basics of garden technique will not only make your gardening experience more productive and rewarding, it will also save money and increase your ability to produce a wider variety of food.

Finished compost is dark in color and has no objectionable odor.

Composting

For the health of your soil and the planet, composting is one of the most valuable techniques available to the gardener. Composting merely takes advantage of the natural process of decomposition that converts organic wastes into nutrient sources for plants, through the activities of beneficial invertebrates, bacteria, and fungi.

Compost contributes to the soil's capacity to hold both air and water because it contains humus. Humus is partially decomposed plant residues, and it both absorbs water and entraps air bubbles, keeping these two essentials readily accessible to crop roots.

Compost also contains varying amounts of major, minor, and trace elements that plants require in relatively small quantities. Because compost is made primarily of plant residues, all the necessary minor and trace elements should be there in their natural proportions. Compost typically is not rich in nitrogen, phosphorus, and potassium, although these nutrient minerals will be present in any type of compost. To meet the nutritional needs of vegetables requires separate fertilization of the garden soil.

A ready-made plastic compost bin will hold about a cubic yard of organic waste.

Compost also introduces bacteria, fungi, and tiny invertebrates to the growing bed. These organisms interact with each other and with plants, reducing complex materials to plant-available forms. This collection of subterranean life also helps to keep harmful organisms at bay, so plants are less affected by pathogens and pests.

Compost and the other soil amendments discussed throughout this book all decompose, ultimately contributing to soil fertility. Thus, if you add compost and organic fertilizers, the soil becomes better and better able to produce vegetables with each passing year. On the other hand, chemical fertilization adds residual salts, resulting in reduced diversity of soil organisms, and eventually the soil becomes unsuitable for crop production.

Compost is made from three ingredients:

- Brown organic matter
- Green organic matter
- Water

Brown organic matter consists of dry, woody materials like fallen leaves. Green matter includes wet materials like vegetable peelings. You should add equal amounts (by weight) of green and brown matter to your compost pile or bin. Chop or shred all additions to the compost for fastest maturation. Water the compost along with the rest of the garden in order to speed along the decomposition process. Locate the compost pile or bin in the shade to facilitate keeping it moist.

Composting, continued

A Compost Pile

The simplest approach to composting is simply to pile everything up, hose it down, and cover it with a tarp. Keep adding materials as you have them available, trying always to maintain equal parts green and brown. When adding green material to the pile, mix it in well to speed decomposition and avoid attracting insects. Keep the pile evenly moist but not wet. Compost will be ready in a couple of months to a year, when the pile becomes dark and crumbly and develops a woodsy aroma.

A compost bin does not have to be an eyesore; this one blends right into the garden.

A Compost Bin

For a regular supply of compost and a tidier composting area, use a compost bin. You can purchase a plastic or wooden bin, or build an enclosure. A three-sided bin, 4 feet (1.2 m) on each side, accommodates about 500 gallons (1893 L) of material.

To make compost in a bin:

1. Place 6 inches (15.25 cm) of brown material in the bottom of the enclosure.

2. Add 2 inches (5 cm) of green material. (As a rule, keep the volume ratio of brown to green around 3:1.)

3. Top the green material with a shovelful of garden soil, preferably with a few earthworms.

4. Mix the materials together thoroughly with a garden fork.

5. Water the compost thoroughly.

6. Turn the compost on a weekly basis.

7. Add new material on top as you have it available.

After a week, the compost should heat up. This is due to furious bacterial activity. Keep adding material, mixing, and watering. Once the compost stops generating heat, it is ready for use. This will take one to four months.

This three-bin composting system handles the waste from two families.

What to Compost

Be careful about incorporating fresh organic matter directly into your growing beds without composting. When undecomposed organic material is added directly to a garden bed, bacterial activity increases dramatically. The rapidly growing microbes will consume all the available nitrogen, leaving none for your vegetables. It is always preferable to produce compost in a separate pile or bin and then add it to the growing space when the decomposition process is complete.

Brown Organic Matter

- Tree bark
- Pruned tree branches
- Dead flower stems
- Dried grass clippings
- Cornstalks
- Shredded newspaper and office paper
- Wood ashes

Green Organic Matter

- Vegetable peelings
- Coffee grounds and filters
- Fresh grass clippings
- Dead weeds
- Eggshells
- Overripe fruit
- Hair, human or animal

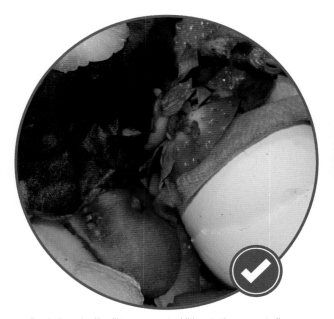

Eggshells and coffee filters are great additions to the compost pile.

Vegetable trimmings are ideal green compost material.

What Not to Compost

- Cooking grease
- Meat
- Dairy products

  (These materials produce unpleasant odors that neighbors may find objectionable, and will attract vermin and flies.)

- Cat litter and other pet wastes

  (These materials can transmit diseases and will attract flies.)

- Human wastes

  (Improper disposal is illegal in most locations, due to the potential for disease transmission and attractiveness to flies.)

- Perennial weeds
- Diseased or pest-infested garden wastes

  (These materials may survive composting and return problems to the garden with the finished compost. Either dispose of these materials in the garbage, or burn them. If burned, the ashes can be added to the compost.)

Don't compost meat products or cooking grease, as they produce odors and attract vermin.

Pet or human wastes should not be composted due to the possibility of disease transmission.

Building a Compost Bin

You can buy plastic compost bins that will hold about 1 cubic yard (1 cubic meter) of compost. If you want to make a lot of compost, your best bet is to build a compost bin. Like most garden projects, this can range from simple to complicated. The design will depend on how much compost you want to make and how you want the bin to look.

Serious gardeners will want a two- or three-bin composting system. Raw materials are added to the first bin, and when it is filled, the compost is turned by transferring it to the second bin. The process is repeated as the compost is moved from the second bin to the third before its application to the garden.

Compost bins should be covered to keep out marauding animals and hold in heat and moisture.

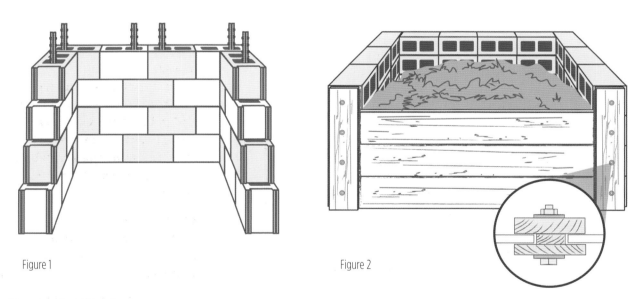

Figure 1

Figure 2

Concrete Blocks

You can make a serviceable compost bin quickly with cinder blocks. Stack the blocks in a U-shaped arrangement (see Figure 1) and use lengths of rebar driven into the ground to keep the blocks from moving around.

For a more convenient arrangement, you can attach wooden battens to the front of the blocks (see Figure 2) and close the front of the bin with lengths of boards, adding boards as you add compost. In this design, the blocks are turned with the holes facing outward to provide ventilation for the bin. This is a better design than the first one, albeit requiring more materials and more work.

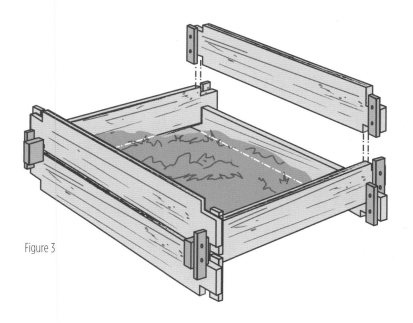

Figure 3

Figure 4

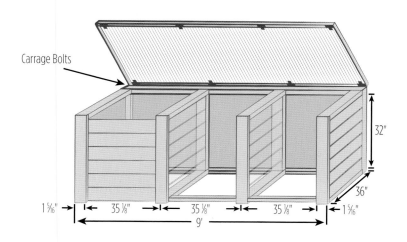

Carrage Bolts

1 ⁵⁄₁₆"   35 ⅛"   35 ⅛"   35 ⅛"   1 ⁵⁄₁₆"

9'

32"

36"

Figure 5

Wood

A professional-grade compost bin or bin system can be made out of wood. Use cypress, cedar, or pressure-treated pine for the bin, which must resist weather and the heavy bacterial activity going on within it.

For the simplest wooden bin possible, see the illustration (Figure 3), which should be self-explanatory.

Exploded diagrams for a single (Figure 4) and triple (Figure 5) bin arrangement are shown here, also. Constructing either one will require considerable time and carpentry skills, not to mention the appropriate tools.

Plants from Cuttings

One of the easiest ways to obtain new plants for the garden is to grow them from cuttings. Not all vegetables lend themselves to this procedure, but many herbs do so. You can even root herb cuttings from the grocery store, provided they are fresh and relatively undamaged.

Among the vegetables, tomatoes lend themselves most readily to cuttings. You can plant early tomato transplants from the garden center, and after they grow somewhat remove suckers from the plant to root for a later crop.

Rooting Cuttings

Regardless of the species being propagated, the simple procedure for rooting cuttings is the same, and can easily be done on your kitchen counter.

Step 1: Select a healthy bunch of herbs at the grocery store, or take the upper 6 to 8 inches (15 to 20 cm) of stem from an existing herb plant.

Step 2: Strip off all the lower leaves from the stem. The top portion should be 2 to 3 inches (5 to 7.5 cm) long or should have only two or three pairs of leaves.

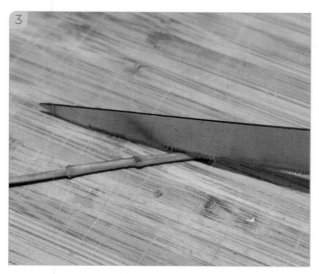

Step 3: With a sharp knife, cut the lower portion of the stem to about 3 inches (7.5 cm).

Step 4: Make sure the cut is at a 45-degree angle. This permits the cutting to absorb water better without its roots.

Step 5: Place the cutting in a glass, with the bottom leafless portion covered with water. Place in indirect light, near an east or west window.

Roots should begin to form in about two weeks. Once they appear, place the cuttings in brighter light, and keep the water level in the glass topped-up to prevent them from drying out.

Some species, such as basil, mint, and tomatoes, will root very quickly. Others with woody stems, such as rosemary, sage, and thyme, will take longer. When the roots are about 2 inches (5 cm) long, you can move the plants to pots to continue their growth. Water and feed the pots as with any other plant.

Starting Plants Indoors

If you have a sunny windowsill, or are willing to invest in an artificial lighting system, you can start many of your vegetables indoors. This not only saves money over what you will pay for, say, a tomato in a 4-inch (10 cm) pot at the garden center. Starting from seed allows you to have plants ready early in the growing season for the earliest harvest. You can also start varieties that are unavailable from your garden center, simply by purchasing the seeds.

While almost anything that will hold water can be used for starting seeds, you will get the best results with good-quality seed trays made for the purpose. The most useful size for vegetable plant production is a tray with 24 to 36 individual compartments or "cells" for seedlings. This size is perfect for growing lettuce, spinach, and other such crops to full transplant size and for germinating all types of vegetable seeds. For larger transplants, such as broccoli, deeper cells about twice the size of germination cells are available. For tomatoes and peppers, when the plants have outgrown the germination cell, they can be moved to 4-inch (10 cm) plastic pots to continue growing until transplant time.

You will also need a growing medium suitable for seedlings. You can purchase a seed-starting mix, or simply sift your regular grow mix through a $1/8$-inch (3 mm) screen. Finely textured seedling mix not only holds extra moisture, but also encourages plenty of healthy roots.

A self-watering system with a humidity dome is depicted in the section on self-watering containers. This type of inexpensive system is ideal for home vegetable-plant production.

Planting a Cell Tray

Step 1: If the tray has been used previously, wash it well in warm, soapy water.

Step 2: Place seed starting mix in a bucket or other container and dampen it slightly with water. This makes it easier to handle.

Step 3: Fill the cell tray completely and evenly with the seed-starting mix.

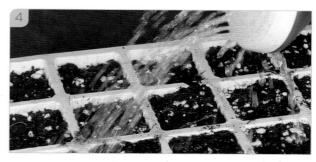

Step 4: Water the tray to settle the mix and dampen it thoroughly.

Step 5: Make a small indentation in each cell with a blunt object.

Step 6: Drop two or three seeds in each cell.

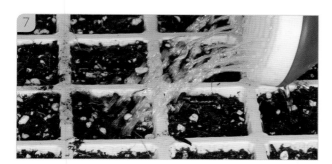

Step 7: Water the tray again to settle in and cover the seeds.

Step 8: Place the cell tray on the self-watering mat in the reservoir and cover with the humidity dome.

Most vegetables will germinate at a temperature between 65°F (18°C) and 75°F (24°C). Expect most seeds to germinate within a week, although peppers, carrots, and some others can take much longer.

Integrated Pest Management

Although integrated pest management, or IPM, was developed for commercial growers, the backyard vegetable gardener can greatly benefit from applying this approach to control plant pests and disease.

Integrated pest management has 10 basic elements. When these elements are integrated, that is, used in concert with each other, the crop is least likely to suffer pest problems. Let's look at each element and what it means for the home gardener.

Soil Preparation

We have repeatedly stated that healthy, unstressed plants are least likely to develop problems. Plant health begins with proper soil preparation. Follow the guidelines given earlier in the book to ensure you have healthy, fertile soil.

Planting

Planting at the proper season is of obvious importance. Less obvious is the need for proper plant spacing and the use of techniques such as intercropping to minimize stress while maximizing productivity.

Forecasting

Pay attention to weather forecasts, along with trends in your specific area. If your region, for example, is subject to late frosts, schedule plantings of warm-season crops well after the likelihood of frost has diminished.

Pest Trapping

Simple traps do the least environmental damage of any form of insect control. Aphids and other sucking insects may be trapped with sticky traps colored yellow, which attracts them. Potato beetles will be foiled by a trench around the potato patch, which acts like the trenches around a military encampment. Hapless beetles fall into the trench, cannot escape, and may then be drowned with the hose.

Monitoring

It seems obvious, but one of the simplest things you can do to manage pests is to check the condition of the plants on a daily basis. The earlier problems are detected, the easier they are to solve.

Thresholds

The idea of thresholds takes into account the life cycle of the pest. For example, pests may be far more locally abundant at one time of the season than at another. Timing crop plantings to coincide with minimal pest populations reduces the likelihood that those populations will reach the necessary threshold number to create an infestation.

Cultural Controls

Culture practices can affect pests significantly. The simplest method is to create a barrier to pest invasion. Covering vulnerable crops with a floating row cover is an example of this.

Biological Controls

The predators and diseases of crop-eating insects can be used against them as natural forms of pest control. We will discuss this in detail in a subsequent section.

Chemical Controls

Certain chemicals are approved for organic gardening, but even these should be considered a last resort. Keeping insects from attacking in the first place should be the priority.

Record Keeping

Keeping a garden journal not only helps with scheduling of pest control applications, it also will guide you in your efforts in future years if you record your results.

Spiders are among the most widespread insect predators and should be welcome in your garden.

Natural Predators

It's a bug-eat-bug world out there. Whenever insect pests find your vegetable crop, chances are their numbers will also attract insects that feed on them. This is one reason to avoid using broad-spectrum chemical pesticides: the good insects are killed along with the bad ones.

While it is impossible to discuss here every helpful insect you might discover in your garden, you should be aware that many of the common ones are there to help, not harm.

Spiders

Spiders are not themselves insects, but are universally among the major predators of insects. Unless there is an arachnophobe in the family, any spiders you discover in the vegetable garden should remain unmolested.

Wasps

Not all wasps sting, although some do and can be aggressive. The majority of the vast wasp family preys upon other insects in a way that suggests a horror movie script. The female wasp either captures an insect and deposits eggs with it in a nest or lays her eggs on a living insect. When the eggs hatch, they consume the prey insect alive, it having been immobilized by paralytic venom from the female's sting.

The praying mantis stalks other insects among plant foliage.

Praying Mantis

The fascinating praying mantis is an ambush predator, lying in wait among the foliage for a hapless beetle or caterpillar to come munching by. When it does, the mantis grabs it with lightning-like speed and then consumes the prey alive. Mantises are sometimes imported into the garden as a means of insect control and in the proper climate will establish themselves. A large Asian species is now a common sight in American gardens.

Ladybug

The ladybugs and their larvae are all voracious predators of many types of sucking insects. As such, they have been treasured by farmers for centuries. It is thought that the name *ladybug* is a reference to Our Lady of the Catholic Church, which sent the insects in response to prayers for rescue of believers' crops. Ladybugs are often sold for release into the garden, but if circumstances are not to their liking they may not remain on the scene for long.

Lacewing

Lacewings are a group of night-flying predators that feed upon many other types of soft-bodied insects. The lacewing larva is such a fearsome beast it may devour its own siblings. Thus, the eggs are placed at the end of long filaments, keeping the larvae as far as possible from each other's hungry jaws.

In Your Garden

All parts of the world have characteristic insect faunas, and many have examples of each of the insect families just discussed. Importation of insects is governed by complex regulations. Seek out advice from a local professional.

Refuge Borders

One of the most delightful ways to encourage natural predators to visit your vegetable garden involves adding a border or bed of flowers. Such a refuge border serves to attract and shelter pollinating insects as well as the predators that come to feed on them. In turn, the pollinators and predators visit your vegetables, assisting with production and pest control. The great benefit of this approach is that it is automatically in tune with the local insect population.

A Separate Space

To be maximally effective, the refuge border should enclose the entire growing area. If your vegetable garden is thoughtfully integrated into the rest of the landscaping around your home, existing ornamental plants may already be helping with pest control. If that is the case, you can enhance the space by adding some of the annual flowers mentioned on the following page. If you garden on a deck or patio, try to make room for a large pot of mixed annual flowers, the best substitute for a full-sized border. If you grow in raised beds, you can also grow annual flowers in one as part of your crop rotation. This is equivalent to letting the bed lie fallow for a year.

A colorful flower border near the vegetable garden attracts both pollinators and predatory insects.

Pollinators attracted to the garden by ornamentals will also visit your vegetable crops.

What to Plant

The best plants for a refuge bed or border have brightly colored, conspicuous flowers, are readily available, and suited to cultivation in your area. Because you want large sweeps of bloom, the most economical way to begin is with annuals that will grow quickly to bloom size from seeds sown in early spring. Here are some possibilities:

Asters

Numerous varieties of aster are grown throughout the world and all of them attract insects with their bright flowers. The aster family is the largest among flowering plants and includes some popular cottage garden species. Among these, cosmos, zinnias, rudbeckias, coneflowers, and sunflowers are almost foolproof for attracting butterflies and bees to the garden.

Basil

The blooms of basil are extremely attractive to bees, and the thick foliage makes a great hiding place for insect predators. Purple-leaved and Thai basil varieties are the most effective for a refuge border or bed. The plants can also do double duty as a source of leaves for the kitchen.

Legumes

Numerous varieties of legumes produce beautiful flowers while enriching the soil with nitrogen. For example, certain snow peas produce bicolor pink and white flowers. Runner bean flowers are bright orange-red, and the poisonous sweet pea is a favorite of floriphiles everywhere, owing to its sweet fragrance. Lupines are also legumes, and their tall, colorful flower spikes beckon to insects.

Copper flashing prevents slugs from reaching this celery plant.

Physical Barriers to Pests

Among the simplest methods for backyard garden-pest control is the use of a simple barrier that prevents pests from reaching your plants to begin with. Depending upon the plant and the pest, different types of barriers will be effective in different situations. Here are some of the most commonly used barrier techniques.

The Death Trench

Some insects simply walk into your garden patch and start eating. Surrounding the growing area with a steep-sided trench about 4 inches (10 cm) deep by 4 inches wide, and lined with black plastic, is an effective deadfall trap for such pests as potato beetles. When you observe captives struggling to escape and unable to scale the smooth plastic, you simply drown them with the hose.

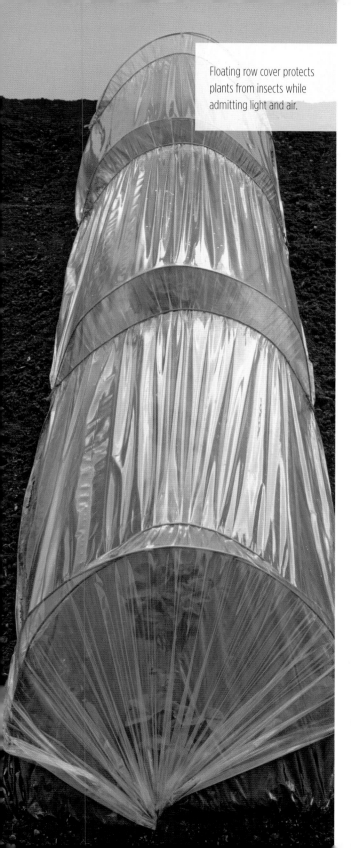

Floating row cover protects plants from insects while admitting light and air.

Slug and Snail Barriers

Slugs and snails are mollusks that can seriously damage all sorts of crops, either by feeding on the mature leaves of lettuces and spinach or by munching tender seedlings of beans and corn. Baits containing ferrous sulfate are effective at killing them, but preventing them from ever reaching your veggies to begin with is the preferable way to deal with the problem. Fortunately, slugs and snails refuse to crawl across anything made of copper. Doing so, it is thought, creates a slight electrical shock that deters the mollusk. You can purchase copper tape about 1 inch (2.5 cm) in width and some small nails. Attaching a strip of copper to the top of your growing bed all the way around will prevent snails and slugs from climbing in. You can also use bare copper wire or copper flashing. Wrap several turns of wire around the base of a pot to protect the plants growing in it. Or set a pot on a piece of copper flashing to hold slugs and snails at bay.

Note that snails and slugs, despite their primitive brains, are persistent and will try to gain access to the pot or bed by devious means. Cover the drain holes in plant containers with plastic or aluminum window screen to deny slugs access. To protect beds from subterranean assault, place poisoned bait on the ground at the base of each side of the bed. Snails and slugs will feed on the bait and die before they can burrow into the bed itself. The effectiveness of all snail and slug baits can be improved by placing the bait atop a small amount of coffee grounds.

Floating Row Covers

Another simple barrier is the floating row cover. This is a long sheet of fabric big enough to go over an entire planting bed. The fabric is woven from synthetic fibers and is lightweight and gauzy in texture, hence the term *floating* row cover. The fabric floats on top of growing plants, shielding them from insect attack. It will also provide a few degrees of frost protection.

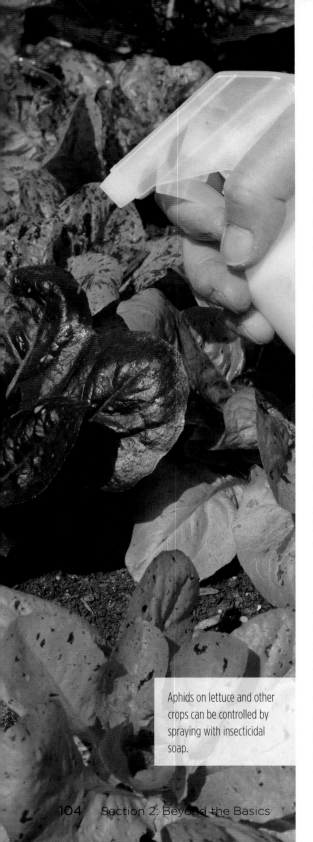

Organic Pesticides

Ever since Rachel Carson's book *Silent Spring* came out in the 1960s, gardeners have been concerned about the dangers of using chemical pesticides to control agricultural pests. Modern organic gardeners eschew both chemical fertilizers and chemical pest controls, but nevertheless have a reasonable arsenal of products that kill insects without harm to plants, people, pets, or the planet.

Insecticidal Soap

Spraying with soap solution can be an effective way to kill many types of insects. The soap breaks down the insect's natural defenses against dehydration, and the bug dies from lack of moisture. Choose a soap made for killing bugs. Household cleaners may contain components that will harm plants.

You can use ordinary household soap to aid in one of the oldest methods of insect control: direct removal. Pick off the bugs by hand and drop them in an empty soup can with a little soapy water. This will dispatch them quickly.

Diatomaceous Earth

An industrial product used for numerous purposes, diatomaceous earth is an effective control for many types of insect pests. It is actually extremely fine particles of silica, produced by trillions of marine algae called *diatoms*. When sprinkled on plants, diatomaceous earth affects insects in two ways. The crystals prevent some insects from chewing leaves, presumably because they damage the insects' mouthparts, and the crystals may also clog the insect respiratory system, asphyxiating them. The product is completely harmless and washes right off the plant like sand.

Dusting cabbage with Bt protects against cabbage worm assaults.

Bt Dust or Spray

Bt is an abbreviation for *Bacillus thuringiensis,* a species of soil bacteria that causes fatal disease in caterpillars. The bacteria are cultured in vats, dehydrated, and mixed with a carrier powder to be dusted or sprayed on crops. Sold under various brand names, Bt is effective against cabbage worms, armyworms, tomato hornworms, and a host of other chewing pests. Repeated application is necessary as rain will wash off the dust, but the product is almost 100 percent effective in controlling some pests.

Neem Oil

Extracted from a tropical tree, neem oil has insecticidal, repellant, and fungicidal properties. It smells a lot like celery, but more intensely. An effective repellant for squash bugs and stink bugs, it also controls powdery mildew and other fungal foliar diseases. It is sold as a concentrate that is diluted and applied with a sprayer.

Spinosad

This is an insect toxin derived from a type of bacterium known as a streptomycete. It targets the insect nervous system but is harmless to birds and mammals. It is effective against many insects and should be used with care.

Pyrethrin

Extracted from a type of chrysanthemum, this natural insecticide is safe for birds and mammals, but is toxic to fish. It is an effective control for many agricultural pests.

Season Extenders

Numerous methods exist for gaining a few weeks on the normal growing season, either at its beginning or its end. Season extenders include anything used for this purpose, from a simple cover to a cold frame. We will discuss two types of cold frames, temporary and permanent, in the next two sections. This section covers some other methods for protecting plants and thwarting Old Man Winter.

Frost damage is evident on these snow pea pods.

Milk Jug Cloches

Anything used to cover individual plants while admitting sunshine is called a *cloche,* in garden parlance. In times past, gardeners who desired out-of-season tomatoes could purchase elaborate cloches made from glass, like a miniature greenhouse for an individual plant. The cost of such cloches has, of course, led gardeners to devise other methods. Among the simplest of cloches is an ordinary plastic milk jug with the bottom cut out. Place the jug over a recent transplant to protect it from late frost. Leave the cap off the jug during the day, and replace it at night to hold in heat.

Tomato Cage and Cover

A wire tomato cage can act as a support for clear plastic film draped over and held down with stones or soil. This produces an effective greenhouse for larger plants. Take care to remove the film on warm, sunny days or the greenhouse may become a death chamber due to excessive heat.

Tunnel Covers

Sometimes it is desirable to cover an entire bed or row of plants to protect them. A tunnel cover provides frost protection without crushing the tender plants beneath. A ready-made cover and its installation are shown in the accompanying illustrations.

The tunnel cover consists of a series of hoops, attached to a synthetic fleece fabric. Typically, the tunnel is about 10 feet (3 m) in length.

Step 1: Begin at one end of the row and insert the first hoop into the soil at the corner of the bed.

Step 2: Stretch out the cover along the bed, and insert each hoop into the soil in its turn.

Step 3: Make sure the cover reaches all the way to the soil line, to inhibit air movement as much as possible.

Step 4: Close the ends of the tunnel with the drawstring, and secure it to the ground with a stake.

Step 5: The finished tunnel can remain on the row until warm weather returns. Enough light will get through the fleece to keep the plants alive.

A Simple Cover for Raised Beds

One of the best ways to gain a month or so of growing season is to convert one or more of your raised beds into a miniature greenhouse by covering it with clear plastic film. The accompanying illustrations show how easy this is to accomplish, using inexpensive PVC pipe and plastic film from the hardware store.

Installing the PVC

PVC pipe is typically sold in lengths of 8 to 10 feet (2.5 to 3 m). These will easily span a raised bed up to 3 feet (1 m) wide with sufficient height to hold the plastic roof well above the plants. Pipe with an inside diameter of $^1/_2$ inch (1.25 cm) is flexible enough for this project.

You have two basic ways to secure the pipe in place. You can simply stick one end of the pipe in the soil, bend it across the bed, and stick the other end in the soil. This will work if the arc is gentle enough that the pipe does not want to escape due to its own elasticity. A more reliable way to anchor it temporarily is to attach short lengths of larger pipe, $^3/_4$ to 1 inch (2 to 2.5 cm) diameter, to the sides of the bed using a metal conduit clamp or strips of plumber's hanger iron (Figure 1). If these are installed before the bed is filled with soil, it will make a neater appearance when the plastic is applied later, but they can also go on the outside and the cover will still work. When the anchors are in place, you simply slip the $^1/_2$-inch (1.25 cm) pipe in the anchor on one side, bend it over the bed, and stick the end in the opposite anchor (Figure 2).

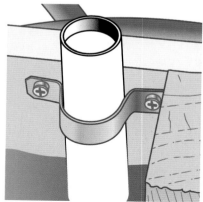

Figure 1

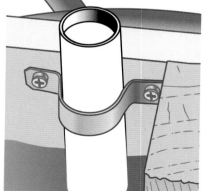

Figure 2

Installing the Plastic Film

With the PVC hoops in place, it is time to install the plastic film. Polyethylene film 6 mils in thickness is sold in rolls in hardware and DIY stores. Typically, the roll is 10 feet (3 m) wide, plenty to cover a 3-foot-wide (1 m) raised bed with hoops. The length of a roll varies. Purchase what is needed for your project.

Attach the film to the bed along one long side, taking care to leave plenty of overlap at the ends to allow you to close them (Figure 3). With the film held in place on one side, it is easy to bring it over the bed and down the other side. If the day is windy, you may need a helper, depending upon the size of the sheet of plastic.

Hold the film down on the sides and ends by weighting it with soil or stones, or fold it upon itself several times and anchor it to one edge of the bed with small nails. Do not permanently attach the other side. You will need to open it to access the bed. Draw the ends together and secure with soil or stones, and the project is complete (Figure 4).

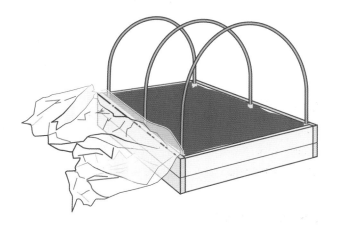

Figure 3

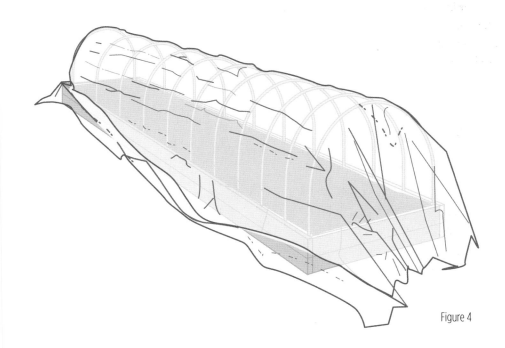

Figure 4

Building a Cold Frame

If you want something more frost protective than the simple covers for raised beds shown in the previous section, you can build a cold frame. A cold frame is an enclosure designed to protect plants from several degrees of frost. It is usually insulated and can be closed almost airtight.

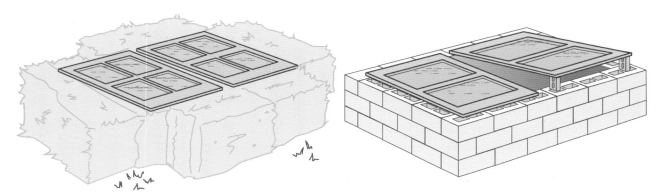

Straw Bales

You can make a cheap, though temporary, cold frame with straw bales and a few old window sashes. This type of cold frame is ideal for starting seeds or for hardening off transplants.

Concrete Blocks

You can also make a cold frame from cinder blocks and window sashes. This is a more permanent arrangement. For extra insulation, fill the holes in the blocks with sand, gravel or soil. Use lengths of rebar to hold the blocks in place or mortar them for a permanent cold frame.

Wood

For a more elegant look as well as an airtight design, build the cold frame out of wooden boards. The back wall should face north, the front wall should face south, and the clear roof should be angled toward the sun. Where winters are severe, the cold frame should be partially buried below ground level for maximum insulation against the cold. In milder areas, the frame can be lined with $1/2$-inch (1.25 cm) foam insulation board or simply left uninsulated.

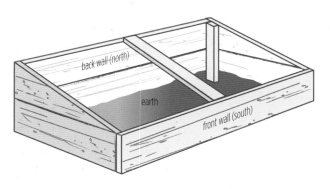

Materials Needed

Lumber

5 pcs	1×12-inch pine or spruce, 6 ft. long
1 pc	2×2-inch fir, 8 ft. long
4 pcs	1×3-inch furring strips, 6 ft. long
4 pcs	lath strips

Hardware

4	3×3-inch steel corner angles with screws
2	3×3-inch steel T-braces with screws
30	No. 10 × 1 1/2-inch FH wood screws
3	3/4 × 3-inch wire nails
4'×6'	6 mil polyethylene film
1/2 gal.	copper naphthanate wood preservative
1 qt.	white paint

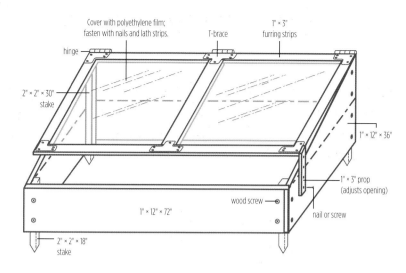

Construction Notes

1. Treat all lumber with 3 coats of copper naphthanate (20%) wood preservative.

2. Paint wood white after treating, if desired.

3. Cold frame may be disassembled and stored after growing season.

Ventilation

On warm or sunny days, the cold frame may work too well, trapping heat and raising the temperature too high for the good of the plants. It is helpful to use a wireless remote thermometer, available at many garden centers and DIY stores, to monitor the temperature inside the frame. Prop the lid open slightly to ventilate the frame and prevent heat buildup.

Automatic openers are available for cold frames. These devices will raise a lid that weighs up to about 15 pounds (7 kg). This is a great convenience if you are not around the house to monitor the cold frame. The cost of the opener is not trivial, but it is money well spent to prevent ruining a whole frame full of plants.

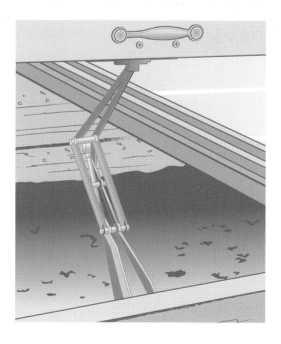

Growing plants indoors under lights offers the chance to grow food almost anywhere.

Artificial Light Gardening

Providing sufficient illumination to grow sun-loving vegetables and herbs indoors is always a challenge without a greenhouse. Although a cold frame will extend the season for many cold-tolerant species, growing a summer crop, such as tomatoes, in one is a stretch except in mild-winter areas.

Gardeners with neither a greenhouse nor a cold frame are thus forced to rely upon artificial lighting for indoor growing. Until recently, the only options were either fluorescent lighting systems or metal halide ones. Each has advantages and disadvantages, but both are rapidly being replaced in the market by LED lighting systems.

Compact, energy-efficient LED light sources are increasingly being used for plant growing.

Fluorescent Lighting

Fluorescent lighting offers the advantages of being inexpensive and widely available, and will be the lighting system of choice for gardeners on a budget. Four-foot (1.2 m) fixtures with two to four lamps each are the best option. Fixtures of lower wattage simply are not bright enough to grow much. The major drawback to fluorescent lighting is the bulkiness of the units, in comparison to the amount of light they provide.

Metal Halide Lighting

Metal halide lighting is widely available for indoor gardening, but has several drawbacks that limit its usefulness, especially in households with children. While the illumination from a single 250-watt metal halide lamp is enough to grow a determinate tomato to maturity and fruition, the lamps get dangerously hot and can explode if water splashes on them. The heat may also make the growing area too warm for the plants without forced-air ventilation, and the lamp wastes much of the energy consumed, both as heat and in non-PAR wavelengths.

LED Lighting

LED lighting systems provide bright illumination in a compact unit that uses very little electricity. For purposes of growing plants, light output from an artificial source is measured in PAR units. *PAR* stands for photosynthetically active radiation. Plants do not utilize the light from the entire visible spectrum but rather take up certain blue and red wavelengths primarily. The amount of light energy emitted in those wavelengths by a given light source is the PAR value of the source.

Because individual LEDs can be tuned precisely to the light frequency they emit, it is possible to design LED lighting systems that provide most of their energy in the wavelengths that plants need to grow. As a result, the productivity of an indoor garden is dramatically increased when LED systems are in use. For example, one 20-watt LED unit can provide as much illumination as a 250-watt metal halide lamp.

The primary drawback to LED systems is their high initial cost.

What to Grow

If you stick with basic LED or fluorescent lighting systems, you can grow virtually any of the leafy greens and annual herbs indoors. With a larger system, you can produce tomatoes and some other fruit crops, provided the cultivars are compact in size. Numerous super compact tomato varieties are available, for example.

Vegetables to Grow

This section explores the world of vegetables, from commonplace ones everyone has eaten, to a few that most people may not have tried yet. Virtually all of them are well suited to cultivation throughout the temperate zone, and many will grow in milder areas as well. Extreme latitudes may limit vegetable production owing to day length issues for some varieties.

Not all varieties of vegetables will be available everywhere. Seek out local knowledge on specific cultivars that are being grown by backyard gardeners. Online social media makes interacting with fellow food gardeners simple.

A summary of "Quick Facts" accompanies each entry and contains information regarding each crop's season of growth, degree of difficulty, crop rotation group, fertilizer demands, amenability to container culture, average days to harvest, and whether the crop can be interplanted.

Vegetables listed as moderately difficult should be attempted after gaining some experience. Vegetables described as difficult are unusually demanding. Crop rotation groups are covered in an earlier section.

Fertilizer-demand facts highlight a vegetable's specific needs in this regard. Most crops will perform acceptably in soils of average fertility. Some need special attention, especially if harvested repeatedly.

Not all vegetables grow well in containers, although some may perform exceptionally well. Gardeners who are limited to container growing should choose varieties appropriately.

Days to harvest for direct-seeded vegetables means the number of days after germination. For plants that are transplanted to the garden from seeds started indoors, the days to harvest is counted from the transplant date.

Interplantability refers to the vegetable's tolerance for close companions. Some combinations are better than others in this regard.

Arugula _(Eruca sativa)_

SEASON
Cool season

DEGREE OF DIFFICULTY
Easy

CROP ROTATION GROUP
Leaves and
Flowers Group

FERTILIZER
Nitrogen

CONTAINER GARDEN
Ideal choice

DAYS TO HARVEST
30-45

INTERPLANTABLE
Yes

Arugula is known also as _roquette_ or _peanut butter plant._ Many people do agree it tastes like peanut butter. This vitamin-rich green needs only a few weeks from seed to harvest, and is often ready to eat within a month. It adapts well to container growing and can be grown to harvestable size indoors under artificial light more quickly than any other leafy green.

Planting

Direct-seed in small amounts, beginning as soon as the soil can be worked in spring. Arugula also makes a fine winter crop for a cold frame. Varieties bred to be cold-tolerant can survive 6°F (-14°C). For variation in both appearance and flavor, sow different selections of seed from different suppliers. Wild arugula, which has smaller leaves with sinuous edges, is an example of such a selection, as are the cold-tolerant forms. Sow seed $^1/_4$ inch (6.35 mm) deep in average soil that has been amended with organic matter. Apply one tablespoon of cottonseed meal per 1 square yard (91.5 square centimeters) of growing area at planting time.

Cultivation

Keep the growing area moist, but not wet. Do not allow plants to wilt. Keep the bed free of weeds. Arugula matures so quickly it will not need additional fertilization. As the weather warms with the progress of the season, arugula will mature more quickly. When you observe that the plants elongate and start making flower buds, it is time to discard them, unless you want seeds. In some areas, arugula will self-sow and establish itself in the garden, saving you the effort of replanting.

Harvesting

Harvest baby arugula when plants are about 3 inches (7.5 cm) tall or allow them to get about twice that size for a more pronounced flavor. Cease harvesting and replace with another crop when the weather heats up. Hot weather will result in a harsh, bitter flavor; indeed, the taste test may be the best way to determine when the crop is finished. Just pinch off a bit of leaf and taste it. If you wish to extend the harvest a bit longer, pick the flowers and add them to salads. They have a flavor similar to the young leaves, though less pronounced.

Follow arugula with beans, or interplant it with peas. The legumes will help restore nitrogen removed from the soil by the fast-growing arugula. If the weather has warmed up, follow with any other crop rotation group besides the leaves and flowers group.

Arugula need not be used solely as an addition to salads. The leaves may be added to soup or made into a pesto-like sauce. They can also substitute for lettuce on a sandwich.

Bean, Green *(Phaseolus vulgaris)*

SEASON
Warm

DEGREE OF DIFFICULTY
Easy

CROP ROTATION GROUP
Legumes Group

FERTILIZER
Not needed

CONTAINER GARDEN
Yes

DAYS TO HARVEST
50-60 (bush), 60-75 (pole)

INTERPLANTABLE
Yes

Green, or snap, beans are highly recommended for beginning vegetable gardeners. Bush bean varieties typically mature in two months or less, provide multiple pickings per planting, and can be planted in succession for a long harvest season. Pole bean varieties mature two weeks or so later than bush beans planted at the same time. They form vigorous vines that can grow 6 to 8 feet (2 to 2.5 m) tall and require a trellis. Pole beans are easier to pick, and produce more pounds per square foot than bush beans do.

Green beans come in many cultivars, ranging from tiny pods the diameter of a pencil to big, flat versions as large as a ruler. There are waxy yellow ones and bright purple ones. Filet or French beans produce pencil-thin pods and come in both bush and pole types. Heirloom beans are usually both well adapted to local conditions and delicious when cooked, and local varieties are worth seeking out.

Planting

Plant beans when the soil temperature has reached 60°F (16°C). In spring, this will typically be 8 to 10 weeks after the last freeze. Beans that mature in cool temperatures have a better flavor, so fall crops taste better than summer crops where summers are hot. Plant fall beans (bush or half-runner types are best) about 10 to 12 weeks before the anticipated first frost.

Bean seeds may rot in cool, wet soil. This is more likely if the seeds are light in color. Therefore, plant dark-seeded varieties in spring and light-seeded ones later in the season. Space seeds of bush varieties about 4 inches (10 cm) apart and 1 inch (2.5 cm) deep, thinning after true leaves appear to stand 8 inches (20 cm) apart.

Beans will grow in almost any soil that is well drained, but do best with a slightly acidic pH of 6.0. Apply a soluble nitrogen source only during the first three weeks of growth. Adding nitrogen for a longer period may actually reduce the crop.

Pole beans need be planted only once per season, as they bear over a long period. Support them with a bamboo or rough-sawn wooden pole about 1 inch (2.5 cm) in diameter and at least 8 feet (2.5 m) tall, sunk firmly into the ground, and spaced about 18 inches (45.75 cm) apart. Sow four or five seeds around the base of each pole. You can also build a teepee of several long poles, their bases arranged around the perimeter of a circle about 6 feet (2 m) in diameter. Leave a gap to enter the teepee from the north side. When the vines are mature, you can pick beans in the cool shade of the teepee or perhaps even grow a small crop of summer lettuce or parsley under there. Children love bean teepees, too.

Cultivation

Beans and other legumes have beneficial bacteria on their roots that supply the plant with nitrogen. You can purchase soil inoculants that jump-start this partnership and increase yield. Just before sowing, combine the inoculant, a little water, and your seeds.

Harvesting

Harvest beans frequently to keep the vines producing. Although different varieties will mature at different pod sizes, in general all green beans should be picked before the individual beans are discernible in the pod. Quality suffers if the pods remain on the vine too long.

Keep freshly picked green beans cool and dry until you are ready to use them. Wet beans will mold quickly. Refrigerate them uncovered and use or preserve them within three days.

Beans interplanted with white sweet alyssum and cilantro (foreground).

Beet (Beta vulgaris)

SEASON
Cool

DEGREE OF DIFFICULTY
Moderate

CROP ROTATION GROUP
Roots Group

FERTILIZER
Phosphorus

CONTAINER GARDEN
Yes

DAYS TO HARVEST
55-60

INTERPLANTABLE
Yes

Beets require little nitrogen, but perform best in soil rich in phosphorus. The soil pH is important for beet production. If it is less than 6.0 add limestone in the fall, or add wood ashes to the planting area. Besides the traditional red varieties, there are yellow beets and an interesting red and white one that resembles a target when sliced.

Planting

Sow seeds $1/2$ inch (1.25 cm) deep directly in the growing bed. Sow about a month before your last frost date. Most varieties require around 60 days to mature a crop. Correct spacing is important for proper root development. Therefore, the key to growing good beets lies in thinning the seedlings to the proper distance before they become too large.

Cultivation

Thin beet seedlings as soon as true leaves appear. Removed plants can be added to salads. Space plants 4 inches (10 cm) apart each way. Keep the bed free of weeds and well irrigated throughout the growing season. If the bed has been properly amended with phosphorus, additional fertilization is not needed.

Beets adapt well to container growing as long as the soil requirements are met. Repeated watering will be necessary, and consequently fertilization, because irrigation flushes out nutrients. About every two weeks apply a balanced organic fertilizer, following the manufacturer's directions for container application.

Beet foliage is highly decorative. The plant thus lends itself to cultivation among ornamental plantings. Plants can be left in the ground and only the leaves harvested for the table. They will resprout throughout the growing season. Beets are biennial, and may overwinter, returning the following spring with additional leaves and eventually a tall flower spike dotted with numerous tiny blooms. The roots of maturing beets, even during the first season, become woody and inedible.

Harvesting

Harvest beets when they are colored-up and have reached the size you want, typically 1 to 2 inches (2.5 to 5 cm) in diameter. Beet leaves are good in salads and can also be cooked and eaten. After harvesting the roots, cut off all but an inch of the tops but leave the taproot intact. Wash off the soil, dry well, and store in plastic bags under refrigeration. Try not to damage the skin, which protects the root against bacteria and mold.

Broccoli *(Brassica oleracea var. botrytis)*

SEASON
Cool

DEGREE OF DIFFICULTY
Moderate

CROP ROTATION GROUP
Leaves and
Flowers Group

FERTILIZER
Nitrogen

CONTAINER GARDEN
Yes

DAYS TO HARVEST
55–75 (broccoli)
50 (broccolini)

INTERPLANTABLE
No

One of the most nutritious crops you can grow, broccoli is not easy to grow in warm-summer areas. Broccoli heads, actually the flowers, need to mature in cool weather. Where the weather heats up quickly in spring, broccoli does best as a fall crop. In mild-winter areas, it can be grown as a winter vegetable. In cool-summer areas, gardeners can produce two crops per year in succession. Besides the familiar heading-broccoli varieties, you can grow broccolini, or sprouting broccoli. This variety has a slightly more bitter flavor. It is cold tolerant and does well as an overwinter crop where temperatures remain above 10°F (12°C). Culture is the same as for broccoli.

Planting

Home gardeners may want to purchase started plants from a reputable garden center, as stress during early life will reduce the productivity of mature broccoli.

Seeds germinate best at 75°F (24°C). Sow 3 seeds in each of several 3-inch (7.5 cm) pots, covering them with $1/4$ inch (6.35 mm) of potting mix. Water well and keep evenly moist throughout development of the seedlings. Provide as much light as possible. When most of the seeds have germinated, select the best one in each

Broccolini (Brassica oleracea var. italica)

pot and cut the others off at ground level with scissors. At this point, the growing temperature can be cooler (60°F/16°C). Use a small fan to maintain good air circulation and promote stocky stem growth.

Transplant to the garden about 60 days before you expect to harvest, when the seedlings have several sets of leaves. Space plants on 12-inch (30.5 cm) centers in raised beds. When the plants are a foot tall, sprinkle a tablespoon of balanced organic fertilizer around the base of each one. Apply a deep mulch of compost or other organic material to protect the shallow roots from heat and to conserve moisture. Irrigate as needed to keep the soil evenly moist but not soggy. Fall crops should be started about three months before the first hard freeze. With broccoli, timing is everything.

Cultivation

Infestation by the cabbage butterfly (*Pieris rapae*) is a serious problem where the pest occurs. Apply a dust containing *Bacillus thuringiensis* (Bt) at transplanting and then weekly thereafter. Reapply after a hard rain. Control aphids with regular sprayings of insecticidal soap. Apply neem oil or pyrethrum dust if you see flea beetle damage. Trap slugs and snails or install a copper barrier, and shield the lower 2 inches (5 cm) of the stem of new transplants with a strip of paper or aluminum foil to thwart cutworms.

Harvesting

Cut broccoli when the head is tight, dark green and without a trace of yellow. After the main head is removed, most varieties will produce small side shoots. Each well-grown plant should produce 2 to 4 pounds (.9 to 1.8 kg) of broccoli.

Freshly harvested broccoli keeps a week under refrigeration. It also freezes well.

Brussels Sprouts *(Brassica oleracea var. gemnifera)*

SEASON
Cool

DEGREE OF DIFFICULTY
Moderate

CROP ROTATION GROUP
Leaves and
Flowers Group

FERTILIZER
Nitrogen

CONTAINER GARDEN
Yes

DAYS TO HARVEST
100-120

INTERPLANTABLE
No

A cool-season crop, Brussels sprouts can be picked over a long season. Warm weather when the sprouts are maturing makes them bitter. Plants are hardy to 0°F (-17°C) and frost improves their flavor. In warm-summer areas, Brussels sprouts grows best as a fall crop. In mild-winter areas, it is a winter vegetable, and where summers are cool, two crops per year can be produced.

Brussels sprouts is one of the many variations on cabbage that have been developed with centuries of cultivation. It is likely that the ancient Romans grew the ancestors of Brussels sprouts, and the variety we would recognize today has been grown in Belgium since the thirteenth century. Modern breeding of this vegetable has focused upon reduced bitterness, increased yield, and nutritional value.

Planting

For fall planting, sow seeds about 120 days before the first hard freeze is expected. For spring transplants, seed must be sown in January. Follow the sowing instructions for broccoli.

Cultivation

Follow the cultural instructions for broccoli. Brussels sprouts get much larger than broccoli plants, and should therefore be spaced about 18 inches (46 cm) apart. Slugs can be a problem for Brussels sprouts, as the mollusks have no compunction against climbing the tall stalk to get at the succulent sprouts. To thwart them, wrap a few turns of bare copper wire loosely around the base of the stalk.

A single Brussels sprout plant can be grown in a large pot. Use a container at least 12 inches (30.5 cm) in diameter. Secure the pot well, as the plant will become top heavy as it begins to bear sprouts. Feed every two weeks with a balanced organic fertilizer and water regularly to keep the soil evenly moist.

Harvesting

Brussels sprouts can be forced to yield all at once by removing the tops of the plants when the lowermost sprouts reach $^3/_4$ inch (1.9 cm) in diameter. This is a good idea when you want a large crop for freezing. For an extended harvest of fresh sprouts, remove the leaf at the base of each sprout when they reach $^1/_2$ inch (1.25 cm) in diameter. Harvest sprouts when they are an inch in diameter. Brussels sprouts will keep about a week in the refrigerator. Plants can also be uprooted and transferred to an unheated, but frost-free, location. Remove all but the top three or four leaves, and set plants upright in a cardboard box. They will keep this way about a month. Brussels sprouts freeze well. Drop them in boiling water for 3 minutes, drain, rinse in cold water, drain well again, and pack into freezer containers.

Growing Tip

Because they are grown for their leaf buds, Brussels sprouts benefit from extra nitrogen. Add a tablespoon of cottonseed meal or a similar organic nitrogen source to the planting hole when transplanting.

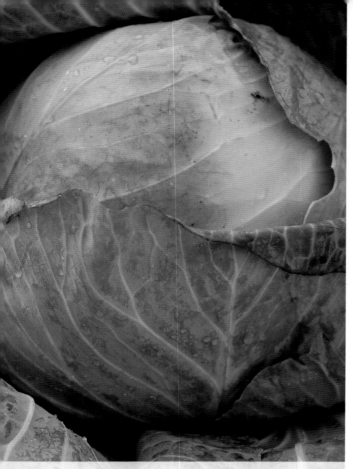

Cabbage
(Brassica oleracea var. capitata)

SEASON Cool	**CONTAINER GARDEN** Yes
DEGREE OF DIFFICULTY Moderate	**DAYS TO HARVEST** 60-90
CROP ROTATION GROUP Leaves and Flowers Group	**INTERPLANTABLE** No
FERTILIZER Nitrogen	

Cabbage is a cool-weather plant. Compared to its relatives, broccoli and cauliflower, cabbage is relatively easy to grow. It needs protection from slugs, cabbage butterflies, and drought. Red-leaved varieties and savoy cabbage, in which the leaves are strongly crinkled, both grow like regular cabbage.

Planting
Cabbage requires fertile, well-drained soil, and should receive an inch (2.5 cm) of water per week. Purchase started plants and space them 12 inches (30.5 cm) in each direction. If you wish to start from seeds, follow the instructions given for broccoli. Early-maturing cabbage, best for spring production, usually needs about 65 days from transplanting. Late cabbage, requiring 90 or more days, is best for fall planting where summers are hot.

Cultivation
Follow the instructions for broccoli. Prevent cabbage from bolting by keeping the soil cool with mulch. Water regularly and consistently if rainfall is insufficient. Periods of drought alternating with abundant water will cause heads to split.

Harvesting
Harvest cabbage when the head has reached the size you expect. This can vary from 2 pounds (.9 kg) to over 10 pounds (4.5 kg). Seed catalogs and packets typically list the average size and days to maturity. As a rule, late-maturing cabbages are the best keepers. Most varieties of cabbage will keep at least a month if kept cold and prevented from drying out.

Chinese Cabbage *(Brassica campestris)*

The Chinese have been cultivating this vegetable for at least a thousand years. It is also called celery cabbage, bok choy, napa cabbage, and several other names.

Basically, there are two types of Chinese cabbage: heading (*B. campestris var. pekinensis*) and non-heading (*B. campestris var. chinensis*). The heading types include the variety usually designated *Chinese cabbage* in grocery stores, together with napa cabbage. The non-heading forms produce loose, upright stalks with smaller leaves. They are usually offered under the name *bok choy*.

Planting
All the Chinese cabbage types should be fall planted. In mild winter areas, production can continue all winter long. Compact varieties are suited to cultivation in cold frames and containers. Sow seeds in cell trays or small pots in late summer for transplanting as the weather cools down. Space plants from 6 to 12 inches (15.25 to 30.5 cm) apart, depending upon the mature size of the variety.

Cultivation
Provide irrigation if rainfall is less than an inch (2.5 cm) a week. Add a balanced organic fertilizer to the planting hole. Feed again after two weeks. Non-heading types mature rapidly and will need only one feeding.

Harvesting
Cut the plant off at soil level. Remove the outer leaves and wash the head in cold water. Drain well and store in the refrigerator, loosely wrapped. Napa cabbage varieties keep a long time under cool, humid conditions.

SEASON
Cool

DEGREE OF DIFFICULTY
Easy

CROP ROTATION GROUP
Leaves and Flowers Group

FERTILIZER
Nitrogen

CONTAINER GARDEN
Yes

DAYS TO HARVEST
40-60

INTERPLANTABLE
Yes

Carrots *(Daucus carota)*

SEASON
Cool

DEGREE OF DIFFICULTY
Easy

CROP ROTATION GROUP
Roots Group

FERTILIZER
Minimal

CONTAINER GARDEN
Yes

DAYS TO HARVEST
60-75

INTERPLANTABLE
Yes

Carrots will grow in little space with minimally fertile soil. Foot-long carrots will require extra-deep soil, but cultivars are available that produce short, fat roots, or baby carrots that develop good color and flavor when only 2 or 3 inches (5 to 7.5 cm) long and half an inch (1.25 cm) in diameter.

Not all carrots are orange. They also come in purple, yellow, red, and white. These unusual color variations are as easy to grow as the more typical carrots.

Planting

Carrots require loose, deep, moisture-retentive soil at least 6 inches (15.25 cm) deeper than the expected length of the carrots. Add rock phosphate powder to the growing area in winter or apply wood ashes in early spring, about a month before planting time. The soil need not be amended with nitrogen. Too much produces hairy roots. Rocks in the soil will cause root deformities.

Soil of insufficient depth will cause roots to bend, fork, or split into multiple points, in any event lowering the cooking quality and reducing yield. Make certain to choose a cultivar based upon the depth of your soil. Sandy soils give excellent results with carrots, as long as there is enough organic matter to retain adequate moisture.

Sow the tiny seeds $\frac{1}{4}$ inch (6.5 mm) deep about a month before the last frost. Crowding reduces the yield by as much as half. Thin young seedlings to 2 inches (5 cm) apart each way when they are about 2 inches tall.

Cultivation

When plants are 4 inches (10 cm) tall, add an layer of organic mulch around them. This helps keep soil evenly moist, important to avoid cracked roots.

Carrots have two major pests. Wireworms can do serious damage. Add wood ashes to the growing area to deter them. Carrot rust fly can be repelled by interplanting carrots with scallions. Do not plant carrots in the spring of the following year, to break the rust fly life cycle. To avoid disease, allow two seasons to pass before planting carrots in the same spot.

Harvesting

Carrots mature on average in about 70 days from germination. Pull plants as needed and cut off the tops. Do not wash the roots. Allow them to dry and gently rub off most of the soil with your hands. Store them in a plastic bag in the refrigerator. Carrots will also keep well if left in the ground. Where winters are bitter, cover them with 4 inches (10 cm) of loose straw to prevent freezing.

Expert Growing Tip

Mix carrot seeds with equal volumes of radish seeds and sand. Sow the seeds together in the same furrow. The radishes will germinate quickly and help break up the soil for the weaker carrot seedlings. Thin the radishes as soon as they appear. By the time the radishes are ready to pull, the carrots should be about the right size for thinning. Pulling the radishes thins the carrots automatically.

Cauliflower *(Brassica oleracea var. botrytis)*

SEASON
Cool

DEGREE OF DIFFICULTY
Difficult

CROP ROTATION GROUP
Leaves and
Flowers Group

FERTILIZER
Balanced

CONTAINER GARDEN
Yes

DAYS TO HARVEST
55-90

INTERPLANTABLE
No

Cauliflower yields a good crop only with difficulty for gardeners outside cool-summer regions. In hot, humid, or arid regions, bringing in a good crop of cauliflower requires both precise timing and good horticultural practices. Colorful varieties of cauliflower have recently become popular, and are grown just like the typical white forms.

Planting
Follow the instructions given for broccoli. Pay attention to seed catalog or packet recommendations. Varieties have been bred both for spring sowing and fall sowing and usually do not do well if grown at the wrong time of year. Maturity time ranges from 60 to 90 days from transplanting.

Cultivation

Cauliflower requires the same treatment as broccoli, cabbage, and other members of the family. Follow the instructions for broccoli. Some varieties of cauliflower require blanching. This is accomplished by gathering the large outer leaves up around the developing head and tying them with twine. This technique produces a white, tender head. Some modern cultivars are self-blanching, saving the effort of tying them up. Catalog listings and seed packets generally mention this feature if the cauliflower is a self-blanching type.

Cauliflower is adaptable to container culture, and indeed, growing it in containers allows the gardener more flexibility in handling the plants. If the weather warms up unexpectedly, you can move the container to a shaded spot for the warmest part of the day. Select a container at least 12 inches (30.5 cm) in diameter, or larger, to accommodate a single plant. Container-grown cauliflower will require watering almost daily, and should be fertilized every two weeks with a balanced organic fertilizer.

Harvesting

Harvest when the heads are tight and the appropriate color for the variety. Avoid harvesting when the heads are wet. Expect a head weighing about 1 to 2 pounds (.9 to 1.8 kg). Cut the entire head and the encircling rosette of leaves. Trim the leaves to a convenient length. Wash the head in cold water, drain well, and store in the refrigerator for about a week. The appearance of dark spots on the head indicates it has reached the limit of its storage time and should be used as soon as possible.

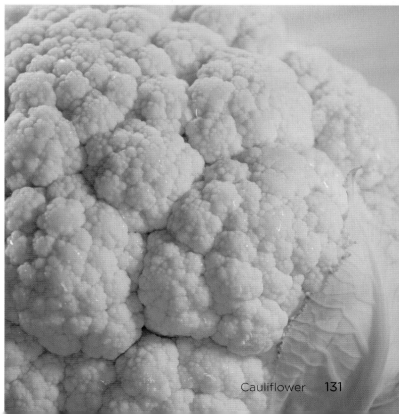

Celery *(Apium graveolens var. dulce)*

SEASON
Cool

DEGREE OF DIFFICULTY
Difficult

CROP ROTATION GROUP
Leaves and
Flowers Group

FERTILIZER
Nitrogen

CONTAINER GARDEN
Yes

DAYS TO HARVEST
85-120

INTERPLANTABLE
No

Celery is a bog plant that matures in about three months. It is grown primarily for the succulent stems and their leaves. A variety known as *cutting celery* is grown only for its leaves, which have an intense celery flavor.

Planting

Sow seeds in flats at 70°F (21°C). Germination may take three weeks. Plants grow slowly and can take a month or more to reach transplant size.

Cultivation

Abundant water is an absolute requirement for success. Celery is a good choice for containers. Container-grown plants can simply be moved around as the season requires, and they will need watering frequently. Regular fertilization with a nitrogen-rich liquid fertilizer will keep the plants growing rapidly. In hot-summer areas, celery benefits from protection from the afternoon sun.

Harvesting

Harvest celery stalks as you need them from the outside of the plant, and leave the rest to continue growing. If hot weather is approaching, harvest the whole plant by cutting it at ground level.

Celery Root *(Apium graveolens var. rapaceum)*

Celery root, or *celeriac,* is grown for the swollen root, which is actually the bulbous base of the stem. It requires a month longer than celery to reach harvestable size, but can be grown with less moisture.

Planting

Start celery root seeds indoors as described for celery. Celery root is slow growing and can take two months to reach a suitable size for transplanting. Sow seeds indoors 60 to 90 days prior to the last frost date for your area.

Cultivation

Grow celery root in a raised bed with other vegetables such as peas, spinach, or onions. Space the started plants 6 inches (15.25 cm) apart each way, in rich, moisture retentive soil. Celery root should receive at least an inch (2.5 cm) of water per week, but does not require constant moisture like celery does. Feed every two weeks with a balanced organic fertilizer. Plants that mature before nighttime temperatures reach 70°F (21°C) will have the best flavor.

Harvesting

Harvest when the roots are about the size of a baseball for best quality. Roots store well in a cool, damp location. Cut the roots away from the swollen portion of the stem, and remove all but a tuft of the leaves. Prepared this way, the roots will keep a month if properly stored. Unlike celery, celery root leaves are too tough to eat. Cutting the root into quarters facilitates peeling the knobby edible portion of the plant.

SEASON
Cool

DEGREE OF DIFFICULTY
Moderate

CROP ROTATION GROUP
Leaves and Flowers Group

FERTILIZER
Nitrogen

CONTAINER GARDEN
Yes

DAYS TO HARVEST
110-120

INTERPLANTABLE
No

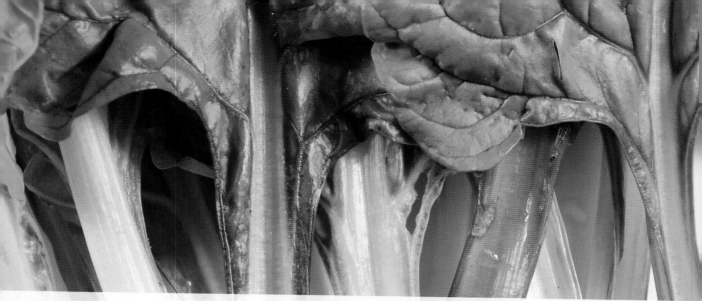

Swiss Chard *(Beta vulgaris var. cicla)*

SEASON
Both

DEGREE OF DIFFICULTY
Easy

CROP ROTATION GROUP
Leaves and
Flowers Group

FERTILIZER
Balanced

CONTAINER GARDEN
Yes

DAYS TO HARVEST
60-60

INTERPLANTABLE
Yes

Swiss chard is a variety of beet that never produces a swollen root. Instead, the succulent stems and leaves are eaten. Swiss chard is well suited to backyard production during cool weather. Some varieties have pure white stalks, but they can be red, yellow, orange, purple, or a combination of colors. The decorative stems and foliage look good "hidden" among ornamental plantings.

Planting
Direct-seed about a month before the last frost in spring, or in late summer for fall planting. Thin to stand 6 inches (15.25 cm) or more apart each way. Swiss chard may also be started in pots and transplanted to the garden when about 3 inches (7.5 cm) tall. Sow seeds in cell trays in late winter. Keep the trays in bright light or under artificial lights.

Pot up to larger containers when the plants are about 3 inches tall. Keep well watered and transplant to the garden about two weeks before the last frost date. If lighting is insufficient, colorful chard varieties will never develop good color. Grow the white-stemmed variety if you have less than ideal indoor growing conditions.

Swiss chard adapts to containers easily and can be interplanted with other leafy green crops. A miniature cultivar exists and is worth seeking out for container cultivation.

Cultivation

You will harvest over a long season, so the plants need plenty of water and fertilizer in order to keep producing. Apply compost or manure tea every two weeks, and irrigate if rainfall is insufficient. Keep the growing area free of weeds, and apply mulch to help keep soil cool and moist. Where winters are mild, Swiss chard will overwinter for a continuing harvest the following season. Eventually, plants will bloom and quality will suffer, however.

Harvesting

Cut stalks at the base of the plant as you need them, and the plant will produce more. Several pounds from each plant is not an unreasonable expectation. You can store freshly harvested chard for a few days in the refrigerator, but it is better to use it immediately after picking.

Collards *(Brassica oleracea var. acephala)*

SEASON
Warm

DEGREE OF DIFFICULTY
Easy

CROP ROTATION GROUP
Leaves and
Flowers Group

FERTILIZER
Balanced

CONTAINER GARDEN
Yes

DAYS TO HARVEST
80

INTERPLANTABLE
No

Often associated with the southern United States, collards differ from their relatives in the cabbage family in that they tolerate heat and heavy clay soils. Like the others, however, collards' best flavor develops when they mature in cooler weather. They are therefore best grown as a fall and winter crop in areas where summers are hot. The large, bold-looking leaves of collards attract attention when they are grown as part of an ornamental planting.

Planting

Sow collard seeds directly in the garden 90 days before the first fall frost. Cover the seeds with about $^1/_4$ inch (6.35 cm) of fine soil and water well. Thin seedlings to stand 12 inches (30.5 cm) apart each way in raised beds. If growing as a spring crop, start transplants in late winter. Follow the instructions for producing broccoli transplants. Insufficient light will produce straggly, thin seedlings. If you do not have bright indoor lighting available, it is wiser to purchase seedlings at a garden center.

When the plants are 6 inches (15.25 cm) tall, move them to a permanent place in the garden, spacing 12 inches (30.5 cm) apart each way. With ample water, the plants can get three feet tall, so place them accordingly. The large leaves look good at the back of a flower border, lending a tropical effect to the scene.

Cultivation

Collards can make do with soil of average fertility, but they do need sufficient moisture. Irrigate if rainfall is less than 1 inch (2.5 cm) per week. For best results, follow the growing instructions for broccoli. Feed plants at transplant time and again about a month later, using a balanced organic fertilizer. When you begin harvesting, follow each harvest with a light feeding to help keep the plant producing. Cabbage worms seldom bother collards, but if you see the white adults fluttering around your garden, spray or dust the plants with a product containing *Bacillus thuringensis*.

Harvesting

Select leaves less than 1 foot (30.5 cm) in length, harvesting as many as you need. Rinse in cold water, drain well, and store in the refrigerator for a week or more.

Corn *(Zea mays)*

SEASON
Warm

DEGREE OF DIFFICULTY
Moderate

CROP ROTATION GROUP
Fruits Group

FERTILIZER
Nitrogen

CONTAINER GARDEN
No

DAYS TO HARVEST
65-90

INTERPLANTABLE
Yes

Nothing tastes quite like sweet corn fresh from the garden. Corn needs considerable space, at least 100 square feet (30.5 square meters), to produce a worthwhile crop. For gardeners with room, homegrown corn is an essential part of the summer garden. Plant breeding has produced corn hybrids that contain much more sugar than traditional corn varieties. The choice of variety, however, is up to you, as they are all grown in the same way.

Planting

Corn requires plenty of nitrogen, water, warmth, and sunshine. Wait until the soil temperature is 65°F (18°C) or warmer before planting or seeds may rot before they sprout. Before planting, amend the soil with compost, cottonseed meal, and a sprinkling of lime. Sow seeds an inch (2.5 cm) deep in hills of two or three seeds. Space the hills about 18 inches (45.75 cm) apart each way, more if you are growing a tall, late-maturing variety. Grow corn in square blocks rather than elongated rows, to facilitate wind pollination. When the plants are 6 inches (15.25 cm) tall, thin to one per hill. Corn can be interplanted with legumes, such as beans, when the plants are at least 1 foot (30.5 cm) tall.

Cultivation

Corn needs abundant water. Keep the soil moist with mulch, which will also help reduce competition from weeds. Remove weeds that grow through the mulch promptly and with care to avoid damaging the roots of the corn. Feed with a balanced organic fertilizer when plants are about a foot tall and again when tassels appear.

Harvesting

Harvest when the silks turn brown and look dry. You can also peel back the shuck and crush a kernel with your thumbnail. If sweet, milky juice exudes, the corn is ready. To extend the harvest, you can plant corn varieties that mature at different times, provided you have space for multiple plantings. If you have limited space and a long growing season, you can often accommodate two early-maturing varieties planted in succession. Average maturity time is around 75 days for yellow cultivars, and 90-100 days for white ones. Expect variation in maturity time depending upon your location and the season's weather.

Non-hybrid corn should be eaten or processed within 24 hours (at most) of picking. Sugar-enhanced hybrids will keep a week under refrigeration but are better if eaten soon after harvest. Freezing is the preferred method for home preservation.

Unfilled ears like the upper one result from incomplete pollination.

Plant breeders have developed compact corn varieties for raised beds.

Cucumber *(Cucumis sativus)*

SEASON
Warm

DEGREE OF DIFFICULTY
Easy

CROP ROTATION GROUP
Fruits Group

FERTILIZER
Balanced

CONTAINER GARDEN
Yes

DAYS TO HARVEST
50-70

INTERPLANTABLE
Yes

The cucumber ranks among the most productive members of the squash family. Pickling types mature at less than 6 inches (15.25 cm) in length, are slightly curved, and often have prickly spines. Slicing cucumbers grow straight, can reach 10 inches (25.5 cm) in length, and usually lack spines. While pickling types can be used fresh, the slicing types do not make good pickles. If you have room for only one, grow a pickling variety.

Planting

Wait until the weather is stable and the soil temperature is above 65°F (18°C) to plant cucumbers. Direct sow five seeds per hill, spacing the bills about 2 feet (61 cm) apart. Add a tablespoon of balanced organic fertilizer to the planting hole. When the seedlings have a pair of true leaves, pinch off the two weakest ones at soil level. Provide a trellis of string, wire, or thin branches for the tendrils to grasp.

Cultivation

Cucumber seedlings need abundant water until they start to climb. After that, they will tolerate some drying. Apply 2 inches (5 cm) or more of mulch to maintain even soil moisture. Fertilize the plants a week after transplanting and again when blooms appear, using a balanced organic fertilizer. Female blooms can be distinguished by the tiny cucumber below the petals. They will appear several days after male blooms form. As blooming begins, start irrigating to maintain ample soil moisture if rainfall is insufficient. Proper watering will prevent misshapen fruits. Water early in the day to permit foliage to dry rapidly in the warming sunshine. Damp foliage is more susceptible to fungal disease. If you have problems with leaf disease in cucumbers, make sure to grow a different variety the following year. This is your best insurance against repeated fungal and virus attacks.

When daytime temperatures exceed 90°F (32°C) cucumber pollen dies. Hot weather may thus result in incompletely pollinated fruits that will be normal near the stem end and shriveled on the blossom end. These fruits should be removed to keep plants producing when the weather returns to cooler temperatures.

Cucumber beetles are a major pest, and are best foiled by covering the growing area with floating row cover. Remove the cover when female flowers appear. Avoiding diseases is a matter rotating with a different crop family, and keeping plants well-watered and fertilized.

Squash bugs may attack cucumber foliage, spreading disease and damaging fruits. Place pieces of cardboard on the ground at the base of the plants. Inspect them early in the morning for squash bugs sheltering underneath. The insects can be brushed off into a bucket of soapy water. Squash bug eggs, which look like little orange-brown barrels, should be destroyed whenever you find them on the undersides of leaves.

Harvesting

To keep plants producing over the longest possible season, pick fruits daily. Fruits that are slightly smaller than the maximum for the variety usually have the best quality. Yellowing fruits are overly mature and should be removed and discarded to encourage more blooms. Expect about 10 pounds (4.5 kg) of fruit from a typical hill.

Cucumbers are most often eaten fresh. The most reliable method for home preservation is pickling.

Edible Flowers (various species)

SEASON
Cool and Warm

DEGREE OF DIFFICULTY
Easy

CROP ROTATION GROUP
Leaves and
Flowers Group

FERTILIZER
Balanced

CONTAINER GARDEN
Yes

DAYS TO HARVEST
Depends upon variety

INTERPLANTABLE
Yes

Backyard gardeners frequently overlook the benefits of including edible flowers in the vegetable garden. Not only are edible flowers attractive and delicious additions to salad or soup, they also attract pollinators and help to dispel the utilitarian look of the vegetable garden. You can use edible flowers to provide a touch of color to beds housing other vegetables or grow them in a bed of their own.

Among the best choices for cool-season blooms are members of the violet family, including perennials such as English violets and the annual pansies and violas (*Viola* species and hybrids). These come in a wide range of colors and are easy to grow while daytime temperatures remain under 80°F (26°C). Other good picks for cool weather are pot marigold (*Calendula* sp.), and nasturtiums (*Tropaeolum majus*). The latter will bloom all season long, as will pinks (*Dianthus* sp.). Among warm-season growers, the flowers of begonia (*Begonia* sp.), gem marigolds (*Tagetes tenuifolia*), salvias (*Salvia* sp.) and daylilies (*Hemerocallis* sp.) can all be eaten.

Planting

Edible flowers can be grown from started plants purchased at the garden center, but many varieties give good results when sown directly. Follow the precise instructions given on the packet of seeds you select, but as a general rule, wait until the average last frost date before sowing. Work balanced organic fertilizer into the top 1 inch (2.5 cm) of the growing bed, using about a tablespoon per 10 square feet (3 square meters). Scatter seeds thinly on the prepared bed and cover with about $^1/_4$ inch (6.5 mm) of fine soil. Thin plants after germination is complete. You can grow multiple types of edible flowers together in the same bed.

Cultivation

Edible flowers will respond well to 1 inch (2.5 cm) of water each week, but they seldom require fertilization during the season. Keep the bed free of weeds. Picking flowers will keep the plants reblooming.

Harvesting

Harvest blooms as they appear. Most are highly perishable, and should be eaten on the day of harvest. If it is necessary to keep them for a day or two, place in an airtight plastic container lined with paper towels, and store in the refrigerator.

Note: Not all flowers are edible. Make certain of your identification before consuming any unfamiliar blooms.

Eggplant *(Solanum melongena)*

SEASON
Warm

DEGREE OF DIFFICULTY
Moderate

CROP ROTATION GROUP
Fruits Group

FERTILIZER
Balanced

CONTAINER GARDEN
Yes

DAYS TO HARVEST
50-80

INTERPLANTABLE
Yes

Eggplant is not as easy to grow as the tomato, to which it is related. Wait to plant until the weather is warm and settled. If started too early, eggplant is likely to be attacked by flea beetles. The leaves of cold-stressed plants become perforated by the voracious beetles. The leaf damage reduces the plant's ability to grow and thus lowers productivity.

In addition to the familiar purple Italian varieties, eggplant comes in pink, white, lavender, orange, green, and striped types as well as elongated hot-dog shapes and nearly spherical forms. Some of the best space-savers are compact varieties intended for harvest as baby eggplant.

Planting

Sow eggplant seeds eight to ten weeks prior to the intended transplant date, which should be at least two weeks after your last spring frost. Wait longer if possible, as eggplant is not deterred by summer heat. Most cultivars require 70 to 90 days from transplanting to begin producing. Two or three plants are sufficient for most households, so you may prefer to purchase started plants from your local garden center.

Transplant to well-drained soil with plenty of organic matter. Cut the bottom from a plastic jug and place it over each seedling, leaving off the cap to provide ventilation. Leave the jugs in place until the foliage looks crowded.

Eggplant adapts well to container growing. Give each plant about 5 gallons (19 L) of growing medium. Smaller cultivars, such as Ichiban, Little Fingers, and Bambino, are best for container growing.

To avoid disease, do not grow eggplant in soil that has grown peppers, potatoes, or tomatoes during the past three years.

Cultivation

At transplanting time, fertilize each plant with a balanced organic fertilizer. Repeat about two weeks later. Cease fertilization as soon as flowers appear or the crop may be reduced.

Despite its preference for warm soil, eggplant tolerates cold well when mature. Plants can be covered to protect them from fall frosts, extending the harvest season by two or three weeks.

Harvesting

Eggplant is ready to harvest when the skin is shiny. Dull-colored fruits are too mature to use. Fruits keep for about three days with refrigeration, and should be eaten soon after picking for best quality.

Belgian endive roots can be brought out of storage and forced as needed, making it an efficient choice for a small-space garden.

Planting

Belgian endive requires 110-130 days of growth to produce mature roots. Since it is desirable for the plants to experience a couple of light frosts before they are dug, count backward beginning a week after your first frost date to determine the best time for planting in your area. Sow seeds $\frac{1}{4}$ inch (6.5 mm) deep in well-prepared soil amended with compost. Into the top 2 inches (5 cm) of soil, work a balanced organic-fertilizer mix prior to sowing. Sow seeds every 3 inches (7.5 cm). When seedlings develop true leaves, thin them to 6 inches (15.25 cm) apart.

Cultivation

Keep the plants well watered. Feed a liquid fertilizer, such as manure tea or fish emulsion, every two weeks until plants are mature.

Harvesting

Cut off the tops and carefully dig up the roots with a garden fork, taking care not to damage the taproot. Trim roots to 6 to 9 inches (15.25 to 22.75 cm) in length. Store the trimmed roots in damp peat moss or sand in the refrigerator until you are ready to force them for eating.

To force sprouts, fill a large flower pot half full with potting mix. Place several roots upright on the potting mix, cover with 6 to 8 inches (15.25 to 20.5 cm) of sand or sawdust and place at 50° to 60°F (10° to 16°C). Keep them well watered. After about three weeks, they are ready to harvest. Uncover and cut the endive leaves. Cover the roots again, and harvest a second crop in three more weeks' time.

Endive, Belgian
(Chicorium intybus)

SEASON	**CONTAINER GARDEN**
Cool	No
DEGREE OF DIFFICULTY	**DAYS TO HARVEST**
Difficult	130-140
CROP ROTATION GROUP	**INTERPLANTABLE**
Leaves and Flowers Group	No
FERTILIZER	
Balanced	

Radicchio plants produce heads in the fall after the tops are cut down. Unlike Belgian endive, radicchio plants are left in the ground to resprout. For this reason, the gardener has less control over the time of harvest.

Planting

Sow seeds directly in the garden about 90 days prior to the first fall frost. Cold weather during maturation improves the flavor of radicchio. Sow seeds $1/4$ inch (6.5 mm) deep in well-prepared soil amended with compost. Into the top 2 inches (5 cm) of soil, work a balanced organic-fertilizer mix prior to sowing. Sow seeds every 3 inches (7.5 cm). When seedlings develop true leaves, thin them to 6 inches (15.25 cm) apart.

Cultivation

Irrigate to provide a minimum of 1 inch (2.54 cm) of water per week. Side dress the plants every two weeks, using a liquid organic fertilizer such as fish emulsion or liquefied seaweed.

Harvesting

At the end of the growing season, remove the outermost leaves to expose the central bud. It will expand in size and become darker in color as the weather gets colder. Harvest as needed, but in any case harvest the entire crop before a hard freeze. Stored in plastic bags in the refrigerator, radicchio keeps about a month.

Raddichio
(Chicorium intybus)

SEASON Cool	**CONTAINER GARDEN** No
DEGREE OF DIFFICULTY Difficult	**DAYS TO HARVEST** 130-140
CROP ROTATION GROUP Leaves and Flowers Group	**INTERPLANTABLE** No
FERTILIZER Balanced	

Endive, Curly *(Chicorium endivia var. crispum)*

SEASON
Cool

DEGREE OF DIFFICULTY
Moderate

CROP ROTATION GROUP
Leaves and
Flowers Group

FERTILIZER
Balanced

CONTAINER GARDEN
Yes

DAYS TO HARVEST
90

INTERPLANTABLE
No

Curly endive is sometimes called frisée, and is a tasty and attractive addition to salad mixes. It does poorly during hot weather and should be grown in spring or fall where summers are hot. In mild-winter areas, grow endive as a winter crop.

Planting

Curly endive is grown like lettuce. Sow seeds $^1/_4$ inch (6.5 mm) deep in well-prepared soil amended with compost. Into the top 2 inches (5 cm) of soil, work a balanced organic-fertilizer mix prior to sowing. Thin plants to stand 8 inches (20.5 cm) apart.

Cultivation

Keep the plants well watered. Feed a balanced organic fertilizer every two weeks until plants are mature. When the plants have made three weeks of growth, tie the outer leaves securely to enclose the head. This procedure, called *blanching,* improves tenderness and flavor while allowing the plants to better withstand heat.

Take care not to permit water to stand in the crown of the leaves as this will encourage rot. Water early in the day so plants dry off before sundown or, better yet, use drip irrigation to deliver water to the roots without wetting the leaves.

Harvesting

Harvest the entire head as needed. Well-grown plants produce heads about 12 inches (30.5 cm) in diameter. Wash well and drain thoroughly. Store the heads in individual plastic bags in the refrigerator. Use the outermost leaves first, and return the head to the refrigerator. It will keep this way for two weeks.

Escarole *(Chicorium endivia var. latifolium)*

Escarole is identical to curly endive in all respects but matures more quickly and produces a head of broad, flat leaves resembling lettuce but with more substance.

Planting
Grow escarole in the same manner as described for curly endive, but allow only 80 days for maturity. Arrange planting time so that the crop will mature during cool weather. Sow seeds $1/4$ inch (6.5 mm) deep in well-prepared soil amended with compost. Into the top 2 inches (5 cm) of soil, work a balanced organic fertilizer mix prior to sowing. Thin plants to stand 8 inches (20.25 cm) apart each way.

Cultivation
Keep the plants well watered. Feed a balanced organic fertilizer every two weeks until plants are mature. It is not necessary to blanch escarole as described for curly endive. The plants will form tight heads on their own.

Take care not to permit water to stand in the crown of the leaves as this will encourage rot. Water early in the day so plants dry off before sundown or, better yet, use drip irrigation to deliver water to the roots without wetting the leaves.

Harvesting
Expect heads about 12 inches (30.5 cm) in diameter. Escarole (and curly endive) can be stored by pulling the entire plant. Wash off the roots, and place in a plastic bag in the refrigerator. Stand the plants upright, if possible. They will keep about two weeks.

SEASON
Cool

DEGREE OF DIFFICULTY
Difficult

CROP ROTATION GROUP
Leaves and
Flowers Group

FERTILIZER
Balanced

CONTAINER GARDEN
No

DAYS TO HARVEST
80

INTERPLANTABLE
No

Kale *(Brassica oleracea var. acephala and B. napus)*

SEASON
Cool

DEGREE OF DIFFICULTY
Easy

CROP ROTATION GROUP
Leaves and
Flowers Group

FERTILIZER
Nitrogen

CONTAINER GARDEN
Yes

DAYS TO HARVEST
30-60

INTERPLANTABLE
Yes

Green kale is the same species and variety as collards. Even when young, kale is generally too tough for use in salad. A related species, Russian kale, is notable for its colorful foliage with pink or red variegation. In all other respects, the two kales are identical. As is the case with other members of the cabbage family, kale is rich in nutrients.

Planting

The culture of kale is similar to the other members of the cabbage family. Direct seed or transplant for early spring or fall and winter harvest. Thin direct-seeded plants to stand 8 to 12 inches (20.5 to 30.5 cm) apart in the bed. Seeds may also be started indoors for transplanting. They germinate best at 75°F (24°C). Sow 3 seeds in each of several 3-inch (7.5 cm) pots, and cover them with $1/4$ inch (6.35 mm) of potting mix. Water well and keep evenly moist throughout development of the seedlings. Provide as much light as possible. When most of the seeds have germinated, select the best one in each pot and cut the others off at ground level with scissors. At this point, the growing temperature can be cooler (60°F/16°C). Use a small fan to maintain good air circulation and promote stocky stem growth.

Transplant to the garden about 60 days before you expect to harvest, when the seedlings have several sets of leaves. Space plants on 12-inch (30.5 cm) centers in raised beds. When the plants are a foot tall, sprinkle a tablespoon of balanced organic fertilizer around the base of each one. Apply a deep mulch of compost or other organic material to protect the shallow roots from heat and to conserve moisture. Irrigate as needed to keep the soil evenly moist but not soggy. Choose varieties bred for the season during which you intend to grow them, as there are spring, fall, and overwintering cultivars. The best timing allows the plants to reach maturity during cool to cold weather.

Cultivation

As with the other cabbage relatives, kale prefers rich, moist soil that has been amended with organic matter. Apply a balanced organic fertilizer at transplanting time, and again about two weeks later. Although cabbage butterflies do not attack kale with the same voraciousness they exhibit toward cabbage, it is wise to keep plants dusted with *Bacillus thuringiensis* (Bt) when daytime temperatures are above 60°F (16°C). Control aphids with regular sprayings of insecticidal soap. Apply neem oil or pyrethrum dust if you see flea beetle damage. Trap slugs and snails, or install a copper barrier to prevent them reaching your crop.

Harvesting

Kale can be harvested at any time after the plants have mature leaves. Clip off individual leaves with scissors, taking only a few from each plant. Multiple pickings are possible. Half a dozen plants will provide regular servings. Cold improves kale's flavor, and some varieties can be harvested from underneath snow cover. Freshly harvested kale should be washed, thoroughly drained, and stored under refrigeration, where it will keep a week or more.

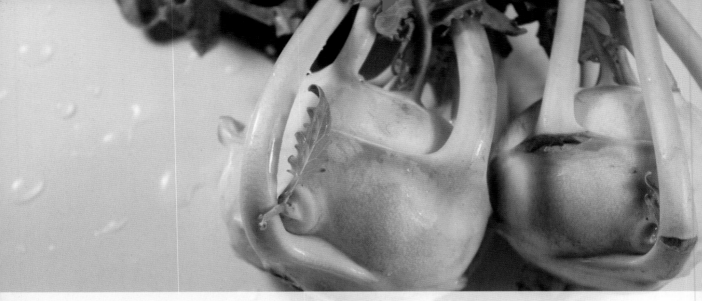

Kohlrabi *(Brassica oleracea var. gongylodes)*

SEASON
Cool

DEGREE OF DIFFICULTY
Moderate

CROP ROTATION GROUP
Leaves and
Flowers Group

FERTILIZER
Balanced

CONTAINER GARDEN
Yes

DAYS TO HARVEST
60-70

INTERPLANTABLE
No

Kohlrabi forms a turnip-like swelling at the base of its leaves. The bulb has a sweet flavor reminiscent of cauliflower, but the plants are much easier to grow. Both pale green and purple forms are available.

Planting

Both early and late varieties of kohlrabi are available, with maturity dates from direct seeding ranging from 60 days to more than twice that long. In areas where the cool season is short, choose the faster-maturing varieties. Where summers are cool, the slower-maturing kohlrabi will get much larger. Sow $1/4$ inch (6.5 mm) deep and thin to stand 6 to 12 inches (15.25 to 30.5 cm) apart each way, depending upon the mature size expected. Plants can also be started indoors for transplant. Seeds germinate best at 75°F (24°C).

Sow 3 seeds in each of several 3-inch (7.5 cm) pots, covering them with $1/4$ inch (6.35 mm) of potting mix. Water well and keep evenly moist throughout development of the seedlings. Provide as much light as possible. When most of the seeds have germinated, select the best one in each pot and cut the others off at ground level with scissors. At this point, the growing temperature can be cooler (60°F/16°C). Use a small fan to maintain good air circulation and promote stocky stem growth.

Transplant to the garden about 60 days before you expect to harvest, when the seedlings have several sets of leaves. Space plants on 12-inch (30.5 cm) centers in raised beds. When the plants are a foot tall, sprinkle a tablespoon of balanced organic fertilizer around the base of each one. Apply a deep mulch of compost or other organic material to protect the shallow roots from heat and to conserve moisture. Irrigate as needed to keep the soil evenly moist but not soggy. Fall crops should be started about three months before the first hard freeze.

Cultivation

Infestation by the cabbage butterfly (*Pieris rapae*) is a serious problem where the pest occurs. Apply a dust containing *Bacillus thuringiensis* at transplanting and then weekly thereafter. Reapply after a hard rain. Control aphids with regular sprayings of insecticidal soap. Apply neem oil or pyrethrum dust if you see flea beetle damage. Trap slugs and snails, or install a copper barrier to prevent them from gaining access to your plants.

Harvesting

Kohlrabi planted in late summer can be left in the ground for harvest all winter, especially if grown in a large cold frame. Harvest when the bulb reaches the size you desire. Kohlrabi stores well under refrigeration if kept in humid conditions.

Leek *(Allium ampeloprasum)*

SEASON
Cool

DEGREE OF DIFFICULTY
Easy

CROP ROTATION GROUP
Roots Group

FERTILIZER
Balanced

CONTAINER GARDEN
No

DAYS TO HARVEST
100-120

INTERPLANTABLE
No

The leek has a delicate, oniony flavor that works well in dishes where regular onions would be overpowering. Leeks require a long growing season, so it's best to start them indoors in late winter for transplanting to the garden in early spring. In summer, additional seeds can be started for a fall crop.

Planting

Sow seeds in a 6-inch (15.25 cm) flower pot filled with any good potting mix. Scatter seeds thinly on top of the soil, cover with a layer of fine soil about $^1/_4$ inch (6.5 mm) deep, and water thoroughly. Place a sheet of glass over the pot to retain moisture. Place the pot in a warm, sunny window or under lights. As soon as many seedlings are visible, remove the glass and keep the pot well watered. Feed every two weeks until you are ready to transplant to the garden, using a liquid vegetable fertilizer.

Thin leeks when they are about ¾ inch (2 cm) in diameter, and use the baby leeks in the kitchen.

Cultivation

The soil for leeks should be deep, rich, and well drained. When ready to transplant, knock the seedling clump out of the pot and separate into individual plants. Trim the roots to about 2 inches (5 cm) long. Trim the tops so the whole plant is 6 to 8 inches (15.25 to 20.5 cm) in length. Set the transplants into a narrow trench about 2 inches (5cm) deep. Space the plants 6 inches (15.25 cm) apart. Draw soil up around them and firm it with your hands. Water well.

As the leeks grow, mound soil around the plants. Try to keep the bottom third buried. Side dress with a balanced organic fertilizer about every two weeks.

Harvesting

Harvest leeks when they are the diameter you desire. Leave them in the ground until you need them. Some varieties tolerate cold well and can be left in the ground all winter.

Elephant Garlic

Elephant garlic is actually a leek grown for its bulb. Cultivation is identical to regular garlic. It will withstand harsh winters. The cloves, four enormous ones per plant, keep for months when stored in dry, dark, and cool conditions.

Lettuce *(Lactuca sativa)*

SEASON
Cool

DEGREE OF DIFFICULTY
Easy

CROP ROTATION GROUP
Leaves and
Flowers Group

FERTILIZER
Nitrogen

CONTAINER GARDEN
Yes

DAYS TO HARVEST
45-60

INTERPLANTABLE
Yes

Lettuce ranks among the best backyard garden crops. It can be grown in beds or containers. Lettuce generally matures within six weeks of sowing.

Hundreds of lettuce varieties exist. Romaine lettuce, also called *cos* is thought to be the most ancient form of the plant. It is also the most nutritious and is more tolerant of warm weather than other types. Others include looseleaf, bibb, and crisphead lettuce. Looseleaf cultivars offer the greatest likelihood of success for the novice gardener. They consist of a rosette of large leaves not wrapped tightly into a head. Bibb lettuce, also called *butterhead,* produces a loosely packed head of soft-textured leaves. Crisphead types make a tight, rounded head of crunchy leaves.

Lettuce is one of the most decorative edible plants. It comes in numerous shades of green, as well as red variegated and speckled forms. Leaf shape runs the gamut from simple rounded leaves to elongated ones to frilly ones. It could easily be included in a curbside bed in front of your house.

Butterhead lettuces have soft, rounded leaves.

Romaine lettuce types are the most heat-tolerant.

Planting

Lettuce seeds can be broadcast directly in the growing bed or you can start them indoors for transplant. Transplant when you want perfect, uniform heads. Use broadcast sowing for "cut and come again" harvesting. Cutting the leaves with scissors and allowing the plants to sprout again from the roots gives you at least two crops from a single planting. The downside, however, is a reduction in plant vigor, and the harvest becomes more perishable.

To start lettuce indoors, fill a 36-cell tray with seed-starting mix, water well, and make a small indentation in the surface of the planting mix with a blunt object, such as the eraser end of a pencil. Drop two or three seeds into each indentation. Lettuce needs light to germinate. Do not cover the seeds, but water gently from the top to settle them in. At 75°F (24°C) lettuce seeds will germinate within 24 hours. They will be ready to transplant when they have two or three sets of leaves and roots are just beginning to appear in the drain holes of the cells. This can take from two to four weeks depending upon the amount of light they receive.

Looseleaf lettuces such as this one are easiest to grow.

Cultivation

Fertilize seedlings with a soluble fertilizer when they are 1 inch (2.5 cm) tall. Avoid exposure to temperatures below 50°F (10°C) during the first three weeks of growth. Harden off plants for a week before transplanting. Transplant with 4 to 6 inches (10 to 15.25 cm) between plants in each direction. Water well. Feed them every two weeks, and irrigate if rainfall is less than 1 inch per week.

Hot weather causes lettuce to turn bitter and bolt or to go to seed. Romaine lettuces are among the most heat-tolerant but generally perform poorly when nighttime temperatures exceed 75°F (24°C). In areas with mild winters, lettuce can be produced as a winter crop. It performs well under cover and will tolerate temperatures down to 20°F (-7°C).

Red leaf coloration in lettuce indicates cold tolerance.

Closely spaced lettuce plants can be harvested with scissors and allowed to resprout.

Harvesting

Lettuce will be ready to harvest about a month to six weeks after transplanting, depending on the variety and growing conditions. Plant a few seeds every week for a continuous supply. You can either harvest whole heads by cutting them off near the base, or pick individual leaves and allow the plant to produce more.

As soon as possible after harvest, immerse lettuce in cold water to chill it and remove soil. Repeated washing in two more changes of water should eliminate all debris. Use a salad spinner to dry the leaves thoroughly, and store in a plastic zipper bag in the refrigerator. Place a paper towel in the bag to absorb excess moisture. Lettuce keeps well for three days when properly stored.

Melons *(Cucumis melo var. reticulatus, C. melo var. cantalupensis)*

SEASON
Cool

DEGREE OF DIFFICULTY
Difficult

CROP ROTATION GROUP
Fruits Group

FERTILIZER
Balanced

CONTAINER GARDEN
Yes

DAYS TO HARVEST
45-60

INTERPLANTABLE
Yes

Succulent, sweet melons are considered fruits by some people, but they are annuals traditionally included in the vegetable patch. The most commonly grown varieties are muskmelons. Cantaloupes are similar, but with smooth skins rather than netted skins like muskmelons.

Planting

Smaller-fruited melon varieties are more amenable to backyard culture than larger types. Sow seeds in hills spaced about 2 feet (61 cm) apart. Place five seeds in each hill. When the plants have produced true leaves, pinch off the two weakest ones at soil level. Melon seeds planted during cool, damp weather will rot before they germinate. Wait until summer has arrived in earnest before planting.

Melons can be grown in a large container outfitted with a suitable trellis. For this purpose, choose the smallest varieties available. Container-grown melons will require frequent watering. Consequently, they will also require regular fertilization. Use a balanced liquid fertilizer.

Cultivation

Melons need loose, fertile, well-drained soil at neutral pH. Soil that is either acid or alkaline will result in a smaller yield. Unless you have room for the plants to sprawl over 100 square feet (30.5 square meters) or so, provide a sturdy trellis. Support fruits as they develop with hammocks made by tying cloth strips to the trellis.

Melon seedlings need abundant water until they start to climb. After that, they will tolerate some drying. Apply 2 inches (5 cm) or more of mulch to maintain even soil moisture. Fertilize the plants a week after transplanting, and again when blooms appear, using a balanced organic fertilizer. (Container grown plants will need more frequent feeding.) Female blooms can be distinguished by the tiny fruit below the petals. They will appear several days after male blooms form.

As blooming begins, start irrigating to maintain ample soil moisture if rainfall is insufficient. Remember that the succulent fruits are composed largely of water. Irrigate early in the day to permit foliage to dry rapidly in the warming sunshine. Damp foliage is more susceptible to fungal disease. If you have problems with leaf disease in melons, make sure to grow a different variety the following year. This is your best insurance against repeated fungal and virus attacks. Neem oil spray is sometimes effective against fungal disease in cucurbit crops.

Harvesting

Harvest melons when the fruit will easily come free from the stem. Mature fruits have a pleasant aroma. Note the days to maturity for the variety you select, and anticipate fruit maturity within one week of that date. Fresh melons will keep several days under refrigeration but should be eaten promptly after harvest. Expect up to six melons per hill of trellised plants.

Sprouts and Microgreens (Various species)

SEASON
All

DEGREE OF DIFFICULTY
Easy

CROP ROTATION GROUP
Not applicable

FERTILIZER
Not needed

CONTAINER GARDEN
Yes

DAYS TO HARVEST
10-15

INTERPLANTABLE
Not applicable

Sprouts and their close relatives, microgreens, taste great, look beautiful on the plate, and are loaded with beneficial phytochemicals. Growing sprouts requires nothing more than a jar, the seeds, and water, while microgreens are grown in trays of soil. Often, the same seeds can be used for either one. Among the many seeds you can sprout are alfalfa, broccoli, and radish. Good choices for growing microgreens include alfalfa, beets, broccoli, sunflower, and wheat.

Planting

To grow sprouts, place two or three teaspoons of the seed in a quart glass jar. Fill with water. Place a piece of cheesecloth over the top and secure it with a rubber band. The next morning, drain and rinse well. Twice each day, rinse the seeds in cold water and drain well. Place the jar in indirect light. When the sprouts begin to develop leaves, move to a brighter location, but out of direct sun. Soon, the leaves will turn deep green.

To grow microgreens, use a finely sifted growing mix placed in a shallow tray or flower pot. Water the mix well, then sprinkle seeds thickly on the soil surface. Cover with more growing medium to a depth about twice the diameter of the seed. Keep well watered and place in bright light. Because the seedlings will be crowded, they will elongate, competing with each other for the available light.

Cultivation

Other than keeping the seeds moist, no further effort is required. Sprouts must be thoroughly drained, to permit oxygen to reach the developing plants and prevent rot. Microgreens need bright light to allow them to develop deep coloration and sturdy stems.

Harvesting

Harvest sprouts when they reach the size you desire and have produced green leaflets. Harvest microgreens when they are about 2 inches (5 cm) tall. Sprouts should be removed from the sprouting container and stored in a sealed plastic bag in the refrigerator. Place a paper towel in the bag to absorb excess moisture. They will keep at least a week in good condition. Microgreens should be cut with scissors at the soil line and used as soon as possible after harvest. They can also be stored like sprouts, but only for a day or two.

Both sprouts and microgreens can be used in salads or as a replacement for lettuce on a sandwich. Sprouts are often added to baked goods to provide additional fiber and nutrition.

Miscellaneous Garden Beans

(Various species)

SEASON Warm	**CONTAINER GARDEN** Yes
DEGREE OF DIFFICULTY Easy	**DAYS TO HARVEST** Variable
CROP ROTATION GROUP Legumes Group	**INTERPLANTABLE** Yes
FERTILIZER Not needed	

Runner Beans

Runner beans (*Phaseolus coccinus*) will fail to bear when the temperature goes above 90°F (32°C). Thus, although it needs a soil temperature of 50°F (10°C) for germination, this bean does best where summers are cool. The orange-red flowers are edible and mature to pods containing huge speckled beans with a flavor all their own. Runner beans will overwinter in mild climates. They need plenty of water, especially when flowers begin to develop.

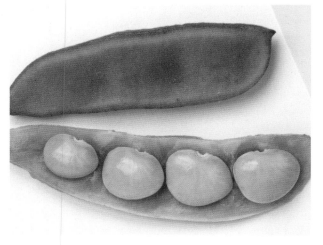

Lima Beans

Lima beans (*Phaseolus lunatus*) require warm weather. The soil temperature should be above 65°F (18°C) before planting. Plant the large seeds about 3 inches (7.5 cm) deep and 12 inches (30.5 cm) apart. Provide a sturdy support, as described for pole types of green beans. Although bush types are advertised, even they require support. Lima beans will tolerate dry soil until flowering begins, at which time they should receive 1 inch (2.5 cm) of water per week. They can be used when the seeds are green, or allowed to mature.

Fava Beans

Fava beans (*Vicia faba*) are grown as an early spring crop, but will overwinter in mild climates. They need a sturdy trellis for the vigorous vines. Plant them in late winter for early spring harvest in hot summer areas. In colder climates, plant in early spring for harvest before the daytime temperature exceeds 70°F (21°C). Pods are usable as green beans when they are about 3 inches (7.5 cm) in length, or can be allowed to mature for dry beans.

Soybeans

Soybeans (*Glycine max*) come in two basic varieties: regular and edamame (eh-dah-mah-may). Backyard production of regular soybeans is not really practical. Edamame is popular in Asian cuisine and is eaten green, with a nutty, sweet flavor. These beans mature at 2 to 5 feet (.5 to 1.5 m) tall, but they do not require support. Plant them when the soil temperature reaches 65°F (18°C). Space the seeds about 2 inches (5 cm) apart in hills spaced 18 inches (45.75 cm) apart each way. Pick when the pods appear to be 80 percent filled with seeds and before they turn yellow. Pods will be ready about a month after the flowers first appear.

Miscellaneous Greens (Various species)

SEASON
Cool

DEGREE OF DIFFICULTY
Easy

CROP ROTATION GROUP
Leaves and
Flowers Group

FERTILIZER
Nitrogen

CONTAINER GARDEN
Yes

DAYS TO HARVEST
Depends upon variety

INTERPLANTABLE
Yes

Miscellaneous greens provide variety and nutrition in salads, and are easy to grow in beds, pots, or tubs.

Dandelion (*Taraxacum officinale*)
The leaves of cultivated dandelion varieties are added to salads. Harvest leaves long before flowers are produced, then dig out the entire plant and start with fresh seed next year. Dandelion is drought tolerant and will grow in any reasonable garden soil. Harvest about 45 days from germination.

Corn Salad (*Valerianella locusta*)
Also known as *mâche* and *lamb's lettuce,* this plant ranks among the hardiest green crops, surviving even at 5°F (-15°C). Where summers are hot, it is grown as a fall and winter crop. Sow seeds thinly in clumps about 6 inches (15.25 cm) apart each way, covering them with $^1/_4$ inch (6.5 mm) of fine soil. Thin to one plant per clump when they have two sets of true leaves. You can transplant the extras to another location, if you have room. Begin harvesting about 30 days after transplanting. Once the daytime temperature reaches 80°F (27°C) the plants will bloom and quality diminishes rapidly.

Miner's Lettuce (*Claytonia perfoliata*)

Native to North America, miner's lettuce acquired its name during the California gold rush. It produces spinach-like greens, and an edible rootstock. The plant grows in any well-drained soil of average fertility. Unlike other green crops, it prefers dappled shade, and will even grow in the deep shade of evergreen trees. Plant seeds in early spring for harvest about 45 days after germination.

Orach (*Atriplex hortensis*)

Orach adds a slightly spicy flavor to salads. Its striking dark red coloration makes it a standout in the garden or on the plate. Sow seeds in early spring or late summer, thinning seedlings to stand 8 inches (20.5 cm) apart. Harvest at the size you prefer.

Purslane (*Portulaca olearacea*)

Purslane contains significant amounts of beneficial omega-3 fatty acids. It is easy to grow during the warm season. Scatter seeds where you want the plants to grow. Purslane tolerates poor, dry soil, though plants grow larger if coddled like other vegetables.

Sorrel (*Rumex acetosa*)

Sorrel is a perennial, but in warm summer areas it can die from water stress. Purchase plants in early spring and establish them in rich, moist, well-drained soil. The flavor is acidic, reminiscent of lemon. One variety sports red veining in the leaves.

Mustard (*Brassica rapa* and *B. juncea*)

SEASON
Cool

DEGREE OF DIFFICULTY
Easy

CROP ROTATION GROUP
Leaves and
Flowers Group

FERTILIZER
Nitrogen

CONTAINER GARDEN
Yes

DAYS TO HARVEST
30-60

INTERPLANTABLE
Yes

Several varieties of mustard are cultivated for their spicy greens. The flavor of this group of plants varies from mild to pungent, depending upon the variety and degree of maturity. Among the numerous types, bekana is mild enough for salads even when mature. Mizuna (*Brassica rapa japonica*) offers the distinct advantage of multiple harvests from a single planting. The tartly flavored, ragged leaves can be cut three or more times. Mustard can sport brilliant red coloration. Tatsoi (*Brassica rapa narinosa*) produces rosettes of dark green leaves. Unlike other mustards it tolerates partial shade.

Mustard varieties are often included in mesclun seed mixes, where they impart a spicy, radish-like flavor. Some mustards have red or bronze leaf coloration. The glossy, metallic-looking leaves add appeal on the salad plate.

Planting

Direct-seed all mustard varieties as soon as the ground can be worked in spring, and again in late summer or fall. Some cultivars have been bred for fall sowing, and these will not do well if sown in spring. Cover seeds with $1/4$ inch (6.5 mm) of fine soil, and keep well watered. Thin seedlings to stand 6 to 8 inches (15.25 to 20.5 cm) apart. Most cultivars mature in around 40 days. Warmer weather will result in harsh flavors and toughness.

Another approach is to sow seeds thickly in a patch. When the plants are a few inches tall, they are harvested by cutting with scissors just above the soil line. Adding fertilizer and watering well readies the patch for another round of growth. Plantings can be harvested two to four times, depending upon weather and the mustard variety.

Cultivation

Mustards will grow in any reasonable garden soil, but do best in organically rich, moisture-retentive soil at approximately neutral pH. Like many leafy green crops, they benefit from added nitrogen. Sprinkle cottonseed meal, alfalfa meal, or another organic nitrogen source on the bed at planting time. Flea beetles can be a problem if the weather becomes warm and dry, but otherwise mustards are seldom bothered by insect pests. Long periods of damp, cloudy weather can encourage attack by mildew, but as a rule mustards are free from disease problems.

Many mustard varieties are extremely cold tolerant and can be grown as a winter crop in milder climate areas.

Harvesting

Begin cutting when the leaves are as large as you like them. If you clip only a few leaves from each plant, most will give multiple crops, especially mizuna. Young, tender leaves can be added to salads, while mature leaves will need to be cooked. The larger mustard varieties are used mostly for cooked greens. Mustards can also be fermented to produce a spicy kimchi, an Asian dish similar to sauerkraut.

Okra (Abelmoschus esculentus)

SEASON
Warm

DEGREE OF DIFFICULTY
Easy

CROP ROTATION GROUP
Fruits Group

FERTILIZER
Balanced

CONTAINER GARDEN
Yes

DAYS TO HARVEST
50-75

INTERPLANTABLE
No

The word *okra* and its other name, *gumbo* are both anglicized versions of African words for this vegetable. Undoubtedly, it has been eaten by humans since prehistoric times.

Planting
Sow directly where the plants will grow when the soil temperature is at least 65°F (18°C), or start indoors for transplanting three weeks after germination. Okra does not require rich soil. In fact, too much soil nitrogen will reduce the yield. Well-drained soil with plenty of organic matter gives the best results. It does poorly in heavy clay soils with poor drainage. Sow seeds about 1 inch (2.5 cm) deep, soaking them overnight before planting in order to hasten germination. Thin plants to stand 12 inches (30.5 cm) apart each way for compact cultivars and twice this distance for larger varieties.

Cultivation

Okra must receive about 1 inch (2.5 cm) of water per week, but needs no fertilization during the growing season. Apply 2 inches (5 cm) of mulch to keep soil evenly moist.

Harvesting

Okra should be ready to harvest about six weeks after germination. Some varieties retain quality as the pods grow larger, but most are at their best when pods remain under 5 inches (12.75 cm) in length. Many varieties of okra have hairy leaves that cause irritation to sensitive skin. Wear long sleeves and gloves when picking. Keep pods picked to keep the plants producing. Okra keeps about three days under refrigeration. If brown spots develop, use immediately or discard. Freezing whole pods is the easiest method of preservation, although okra also makes good pickles.

Okra   171

Storage Onions *(Allium cepa)*

SEASON
Cool or Warm

DEGREE OF DIFFICULTY
Easy

CROP ROTATION GROUP
Roots Group

FERTILIZER
Balanced

CONTAINER GARDEN
No

DAYS TO HARVEST
80-120

INTERPLANTABLE
No

Bulb-forming storage onions include day-neutral, long-day and short-day types. The timing of bulb formation depends upon the length of the day. This has obvious implications for their cultivation, depending on your latitude. Short-day onions start making bulbs when the days are 11 to 12 hours long. Short-day onions are planted in fall for harvest around June. They are typically grown only in mild-winter areas.

Long-day onions form bulbs as the days reach fifteen to sixteen hours in length. They are planted in early spring to produce bulbs during the extended days of summer.

Plant breeders have developed onion hybrids that are day neutral. These will produce a bulb when the days are 12 to 14 hours long, and are suitable for spring planting in most latitudes.

If you plant the wrong type of onion for your area, fear not. They can be used even if no bulb is produced.

Planting

Storage onions require rich, sandy soil amended with compost. Purchase onion sets at the proper planting time for the variety you choose, and press them into the soil, leaving the top barely exposed, about 3 inches (7.5 cm) apart each way.

Cultivation

Keep onions well-watered and feed monthly with a balanced organic fertilizer. Weeding is the most important part of maintaining an onion patch. Allowing weeds to grow among the plants will reduce yield by as much as half.

Onions are subject to a number of diseases, but these tend to be localized. Commercial-scale plantings are more susceptible than backyard crops, apparently. If disease does strike your onion crop, it is wise to seek out professional advice. In the case of some viral diseases, the only option is to destroy the crop and avoid planting onions for a season or two.

Insect pests of onions mostly attack the stored bulbs.

Harvesting

Pull onions when the majority of the tops have fallen over. After harvest, cure the onions in a dry, airy, partially shaded spot for two weeks or until the tops are completely dried. Trim and store in a cool, dry place in the dark. Keeping quality varies with the variety, so read seed catalog descriptions carefully or inquire at your local garden center. Sweeter short-day onions do not store as well as the more pungent long-day types. Day-neutral onions are also sweet and do not store well.

Peas, Field *(Vigna unguiculata, V. unguiculata var. sesquipedale, and V. unguiculata unguiculata)*

SEASON
Cool

DEGREE OF DIFFICULTY
Easy

CROP ROTATION GROUP
Legumes Group

FERTILIZER
Balanced

CONTAINER GARDEN
No

DAYS TO HARVEST
100-120

INTERPLANTABLE
No

This group of legumes goes by a variety of names: Southern peas, cowpeas, field peas, crowder peas, and black-eyed peas. They will grow in poor soil and with little water and have come to be synonymous with the cooking of the southern United States. Asian long beans, or asparagus beans, are of the same botanical species and require the same care. They are harvested when the green pods are about 12 inches (30.5 cm) in length, although they will get much longer.

Planting

These legumes should be planted when the soil temperature is above 65°F (18°C). Seed will rot in cold soil. As with other legumes, soil fertility is not a big issue and even heavy clay soil is tolerated. Nevertheless, the plants will be most productive in organically amended garden soil suitable for more demanding crops. Plant seeds in groups of five, 1 inch (2.5 cm) deep and 1 inch apart. Thin to three plants per hill when true leaves appear. Space hills about 12 inches (30.5 cm) apart. Long beans need a wider spacing, about 2 feet (61 cm).

Cultivation

Don't worry about irrigating these peas until flowers appear; then give them 1 inch (2.5 cm) of water a week. Hold off on the fertilizer, too; extra nitrogen prevents plants from setting pods. If you grow Asian long beans, they will require a sturdy trellis at least 6 feet (2 m) tall to accommodate their vigorous vines. Although the beans will get a yard (.9 m) or more in length, they are best at about 1 foot (30 cm).

Harvesting

Field peas are ready to harvest in about 60 to 70 days from germination. Pods should be left on the vine to dry and then shelled. To shell, place the pods in an old pillowcase. Grasp the top to keep it closed and bash the pods against a convenient wall or tree several times. You can also tie the pillowcase closed with a piece of string, and roll over the pods with a rolling pin. Empty the pillowcase onto a shallow tray and separate the peas by blowing the broken pods away with a small fan. Shelled peas can be boiled for immediate use, canned, frozen, or stored dry. Asian long beans take about 75 to 90 days for maturity, and should be harvested when less than 12 inches (30.5 cm) in length, although they will get much longer.

Peas, Shelling *(Pisum sativum)*

SEASON
Cool

DEGREE OF DIFFICULTY
Easy

CROP ROTATION GROUP
Legumes Group

FERTILIZER
Not needed

CONTAINER GARDEN
Yes

DAYS TO HARVEST
60-70

INTERPLANTABLE
Yes

Fresh shelling peas can be hard to find at the supermarket. Frozen or canned shelled peas have taken over, and the only way you are likely to be able to enjoy them freshly picked is to grow them yourself. Shelling peas are sometimes called English peas. They are easy to grow, but snap and snow peas, which are otherwise identical, are more productive per square foot.

Planting

Peas do not perform well once the temperature rises above 80°F (27°C). Plant them as early in spring as the ground can be worked. They can also be started in a cold frame in winter for the earliest possible harvest in spring. Fall-planted peas may be damaged by an early frost. Although the vines resist cold, the pods may be ruined if they freeze. Mid-July is the typical time for fall plantings.

Cultivation

Peas need well-drained soil with plenty of phosphorus and potassium but little nitrogen. Too much nitrogen can actually reduce the yield. Bone meal or wood ashes can be added to the growing bed to improve conditions for peas. Ideally, this is done in fall before spring planting. Sow seeds in rows about 1 inch (2.5 cm) deep and 1 inch apart. Space rows 18 inches (45.75 cm) apart in the bed. Before they begin to climb, thin them to 2 inches (5 cm) apart.

Provide support for the plants. Peas climb by means of tendrils that prefer to wrap around a thin support. You can use thin bamboo stakes, tree limbs with many small branches, or nylon trellis netting supported on a frame. Even pea varieties that claim not to require support should be given a trellis. Otherwise, they will take up more space in the bed than is necessary. Unless the soil is quite dry as pods are developing, peas seldom need irrigation. In soil of average fertility, peas need no additional feeding during the growing season.

Because they are legumes, peas add nitrogen to the soil as they grow. They are therefore good candidates for interplanting with spinach or lettuce. Follow peas with cucumbers. Planting the cucumbers when the peas bloom should result in climbing cucumber vines by the time the last peas are picked.

Harvesting

Pick peas as soon as the pods are filled out. A well-grown row of shelling peas can produce a pound per foot. Although shelled peas can be preserved by canning, they are much better when frozen. Process them within two hours of harvest for the best flavor, as the sugars in the pod quickly convert to starch after picking. Drop the shelled peas into boiling water for three minutes, drain well, and plunge into cold water to stop the cooking. Drain well again and pack into labeled freezer containers.

Pea shoots and flowers can also be eaten. If a frost threatens and you have picked all the mature pods, the outer few inches (cm) of the vine can be harvested and used as a vegetable. Stir-frying is the most common way to prepare pea shoots.

Peas, Shelling

Peas, Snow and Snap *(Pisum sativum)*

SEASON
Cool

DEGREE OF DIFFICULTY
Easy

CROP ROTATION GROUP
Legumes Group

FERTILIZER
Not needed

CONTAINER GARDEN
Yes

DAYS TO HARVEST
60-70

INTERPLANTABLE
Yes

Although they are grown like shelling peas, snap and snow pea varieties can be eaten pod and all. Snow peas should be harvested before the seeds begin to swell the pod. Snap peas can be harvested at any stage, but those with mature seeds should be shelled out, as the pods become tough as they mature. Either of these crops provide good value to the home gardener, as the weight of the harvest per foot of row is about double that of shelling peas.

Planting

Snap and snow peas do not perform well once the temperature rises above 80°F (27°C). Plant them as early in spring as the ground can be worked. Snow peas are cold tolerant and often do best as a fall crop. Fall-planted snap peas may be damaged by an early frost. Although the vines resist cold, the pods may be ruined if they freeze. Mid-July is the typical time for fall plantings of either variety.

Cultivation

Well-drained soil with plenty of phosphorus and potassium, but little nitrogen, is the best medium for both snow and snap peas. Amending the soil with bone meal and/or wood ashes in fall before a spring planting is recommended. Too much nitrogen can actually reduce the yield. Sow seeds in hills, placing them about 1 inch (2.5 cm) deep and 1 inch apart. Space hills 18 inches (45.75 cm) apart in the bed. Before they begin to climb, thin them to 2 inches (5 cm) apart.

Provide support for the plants. Snow and snap peas usually provide several pickings, and do very well if supported on a teepee of thin bamboo stakes or a metal cage support. Vines can climb to 6 feet (2 m) or more, so plan accordingly. Peas seldom need irrigation, except as the pods are developing. Once blooms appear, give them about 1 inch (2.5 cm) of water per week. In soil of average fertility, peas need no additional feeding during the growing season.

Snow and snap peas can be interplanted with a variety of other crops. Because they are legumes, peas actually contribute more nitrogen to the soil than they use. Interplanting with spinach, carrots, lettuce, or onions gives good results. You can also sow cucumber seeds at the base of the pea vines at about the time blooms appear. By the time the peas are done, the cucumbers will be climbing the trellis.

Harvesting

Snow and snap peas can produce 2 pounds (1 kg) or more per hill. They are best eaten when freshly picked, as they respond better to commercial processing than to home preservation techniques. Many people enjoy snap peas raw in salads.

Peppers, Hot (*Capsicum annuum, C. chinense, C. baccatum*, and numerous hybrids)

SEASON
Warm

DEGREE OF DIFFICULTY
Moderate

CROP ROTATION GROUP
Fruits Group

FERTILIZER
Balanced

CONTAINER GARDEN
Yes

DAYS TO HARVEST
70-90

INTERPLANTABLE
Yes

Hot peppers are easily grown in soil of average fertility. All types, from the relatively mild jalapeño to the fiery habañero, have the same basic requirements. Hot pepper plants are decorative enough to include in ornamental beds.

Planting

Hot peppers require warm soil, humidity, and good air circulation to perform well. In particular, do not make the mistake of planting them too early. While mature peppers can tolerate cold short of an actual frost, the seedlings may be stunted if they are not kept warm. About a month after your last spring frost, sow seeds in individual small pots and keep them in a warm, brightly illuminated area.

Water the seedlings with lukewarm water, and feed with a balanced soluble fertilizer every two weeks, beginning when the first true leaves have appeared. When the plants have several sets of true leaves, in about a month, transplant to the garden. Set plants about 12 to 18 inches (30.5 to 45.75 cm) apart in blocks rather than rows. Keeping the plants grouped together maintains humidity and promotes pollination. Peppers are self-fertile.

Cultivation

Keep the growing area free of weeds and apply a balanced liquid fertilizer every two weeks as plants are developing. Mulch the soil to maintain even moisture and keep mud from splashing on the leaves. Stop feeding when you see flower buds. Too much nitrogen after that point will cause blossoms to drop. Hot peppers need about 70 to 90 days to reach maturity, although they can be harvested when green.

Small hot pepper varieties will grow in a 12-inch (30.5 cm) pot. Large chili peppers will require a 5-gallon (19-liter) container. Container peppers need close attention to avoid dry soil.

Harvesting

Harvest peppers as needed. Hot peppers may yield in great abundance under good conditions. As a rule, the smaller the fruits, the more per plant.

You can uproot pepper plants before frost kills them and store with the roots immersed in a bucket of water in a protected, lightly shaded spot. They will keep this way for about a month and will continue to ripen. Small pepper plants in containers can be overwintered in a sunny spot and returned to the garden in spring.

Fresh peppers are easy to freeze. Small hot peppers can be strung together with a needle and thread, like a string of beads, and hung up in a warm, airy place to dry. When the peppers are wrinkled and rattle when shaken, transfer them to an airtight container.

Peppers, Sweet *(Capsicum annuum, C. chinense, C. baccatum,* and numerous hybrids)

SEASON
Warm

DEGREE OF DIFFICULTY
Moderate

CROP ROTATION GROUP
Fruits Group

FERTILIZER
Balanced

CONTAINER GARDEN
Yes

DAYS TO HARVEST
70-90

INTERPLANTABLE
Yes

Growing good peppers is relatively easy in soil of average fertility. Sweet peppers can be used at all stages, from immature to fully ripe, and thus provide a steady crop over a long season. Elongated types, often called banana peppers, are the easiest to grow, while sweet bell peppers are less forgiving.

Planting

Start sweet pepper seeds in cell trays about 8 to 10 weeks before the last spring frost. Soil temperature must be above 75°F (24°C) for good germination. Cool temperatures and excess moisture will lead to poor germination and damping off of seedlings.

When seedlings have two pairs of true leaves, transplant them to small individual pots. Take care to keep them warm. Nighttime temperatures should not be below 65°F (18°C). Irrigate them with warm water. Never allow plants to wilt. When the outside soil temperature is at least 65°F (18°C), you can move them to the garden.

Cultivation

Sprinkle a tablespoon of cottonseed meal and a tablespoon of bone meal into the bottom of the planting hole, cover with a little soil, and set the plants in place. Space them 18 inches (45.75 cm) apart in all directions. Add a sturdy stake to support the plants later when fruits set.

Feed growing plants with a liquid fertilizer, such as fish emulsion, every two weeks until flower buds appear. Too-low humidity can reduce fruit set. Therefore, plant in blocks of four plants, allowing them to create their own microclimate. Keep sweet peppers free of weeds.

Peppers adapt readily to container culture. Sweet peppers need a 5-gallon (9-liter) container per plant. They are excellent candidates for self-watering containers.

Harvesting

Harvest peppers as needed. The time to maturity indicated on the seed packet or in the catalog listing is the time necessary for the fruits to reach the green stage. Ripening typically requires another month. Expect 6 to 10 fruits or more from sweet bell peppers, more from elongated types.

Fresh peppers are easy to freeze. Simply wash, trim, and cut into convenient-size pieces. Place in freezer containers and store in the freezer.

Potato *(Solanum tuberosum)*

SEASON
Cool

DEGREE OF DIFFICULTY
Easy

CROP ROTATION GROUP
Roots Group

FERTILIZER
Balanced

CONTAINER GARDEN
Yes

DAYS TO HARVEST
65-120

INTERPLANTABLE
No

Potatoes take up a lot of space, but the homegrown flavor encourages gardeners to plant them every year. Unlike most vegetables, they prefer acidic soil, so avoid lime or wood ashes in the potato patch.

Planting

Potatoes are grown from seed tubers. Purchase certified virus-free seed. Plant small whole ones, or cut bigger ones into pieces larger than an egg. Each piece should have two eyes. Approximately two weeks before the anticipated last frost, plant 12 inches (30.5 cm) apart each way and 3 to 4 inches (7.5 to 10 cm) deep. Sprinkle about a tablespoon of balanced organic fertilizer in the bottom of each planting hole.

Cultivation

When potatoes reach 6 inches (15.25 cm) tall, pile soil on them so that only about 1 inch (2.5 cm) of leaves protrudes above the surface. When another 6 inches of growth has developed, again bury all but the uppermost 1 inch. This increases yield, because the crop forms in the area above the seed tuber and below the soil line. Irrigate if rainfall does not provide at least 1 inch of water per week.

Harvesting

When blooms appear, you can harvest a few new potatoes. With your fingers, carefully explore under the plants, taking only one or two tubers from each. When the plants turn yellow and begin to collapse, it is time to harvest mature potatoes. Dig and handle them carefully to avoid injuries that invite rot. Spread freshly dug potatoes out in a dry, shady place for a day or two to cure, then store them in a cool, dark location.

Potato, Sweet (Ipomea batata)

SEASON
Warm

DEGREE OF DIFFICULTY
Easy

CROP ROTATION GROUP
Roots Group

FERTILIZER
Not required

CONTAINER GARDEN
No

DAYS TO HARVEST
100-120

INTERPLANTABLE
No

The sweet potato is a member of the morning glory family, and was first domesticated in the New World centuries ago. Sweet potato seeds give variable results, and virtually all sweet potatoes are started from small plants, called *slips.* These in turn are sprouted from stored roots. It is necessary to purchase slips from a commercial grower to ensure the best quality. Nevertheless, home gardeners can successfully produce slips from purchased sweet potato roots.

Approximately two months prior to the anticipated planting date, place a healthy-looking sweet potato root into a wide-mouth jar tall enough to hold the root up on one of its pointed ends. Add a small amount of water, 1 to 2 inches (2.5 to 5 cm). Set the jar in a warm place with bright indirect light. Maintain the water level in the jar and in about two weeks leaves should begin to emerge from the eyes on the root. The new shoots will grow rapidly and extend their own string-like roots into the water. When several shoots are well rooted, carefully detach them and pot them in small pots. When roots appear in the drainage holes of the pots, they are ready to transplant to the garden.

Sweet potato sprouts will produce new plants when detached from the mother root.

Planting

Transplant slips after the ground has warmed to 65°F (18°C) into loose, sandy loam with plenty of organic matter. High nitrogen content in the soil will result in poor root development. Space individual plants at least 12 inches (30.5 cm) apart each way. The vines of standard varieties are vigorous and sprawling, but for limited-space gardens there are compact varieties that remain inbounds.

Cultivation

Provide 1 inch (2.5 cm) of water per week. As soon as plants begin to run, mulch to control weeds and maintain even moisture at the roots. In cooler climates, black plastic sheeting is a desirable mulch. Applied several weeks before planting time, it absorbs solar heat and warms the soil. Do not apply fertilizer, as this reduces yield.

Harvesting

Each slip should produce 5 to 10 pounds (2.25 to 4.5 kg) of roots if the season has been favorable. Harvest as needed as long as the weather remains mild. Dig all the roots before frost kills the vines or their keeping quality will be seriously impaired. Spread freshly dug potatoes in a shady spot to cure for a day or two, then gently brush off most of the soil. Store cured potatoes in a cool, dry place. They should keep about three to six months.

Pumpkin
(Cucurbita pepo, C. maxima)

SEASON Warm	**CONTAINER GARDEN** No
DEGREE OF DIFFICULTY Moderate	**DAYS TO HARVEST** 100-120
CROP ROTATION GROUP Fruits Group	**INTERPLANTABLE** No
FERTILIZER Balanced	

Pumpkins produce vigorous vines that sprawl over a large area, and are a poor choice for gardens where space is a limiting factor. Better results will be had with winter squashes. Pumpkins intended for jack-o-lanterns are *C. pepo*, while those grown for eating are *C. maxima* or *C. moschata*.

Backyard gardeners are likely to have the best pumpkin crop from varieties intended for eating. These produce smaller fruits, some as small as a softball, and typically have a more compact growth habit. They are also sweeter, having been bred for the table rather than for carving.

Planting

Plant pumpkin seeds in hills, spaced 2 feet (61 cm) apart each way, after the soil has thoroughly warmed up and the weather is settled. Amend the soil with organic matter. Pumpkins require rich, sandy soil to perform best. Place five seeds per hill, and water well. When the plants have true leaves, thin to two or three per hill. Apply mulch, or grow on black plastic as described for sweet potatoes.

Pumpkin seeds can be started in biodegradable peat pots, about two weeks before the anticipated planting date. Small seedlings are most susceptible to insect damage and soil pathogens, both prevented by starting the seeds in pots. Cover the seeds with half an inch of fine growing medium and water well. Expect germination in about a week. Biodegradable pots are necessary to avoid disturbing the roots when transplanting. The entire pot is buried without removing the plants.

Cultivation

Keep plants well watered throughout the growing season, and feed a balanced organic fertilizer every two weeks until the blooms appear. Remove weeds from the growing area as they appear. Cultivate carefully to avoid damaging the roots. Pumpkins are heavy feeders and their growth should not be interrupted during the season by a lack of food or water.

Fungal diseases and insect pests may attack pumpkins. These problems are best avoided by proper cultivation, and in particular by growing the plants in a warm, sunny location. Neem oil can be an effective control for mildew, and it also repels the squash bug. These are the two most likely problems.

Harvesting

Pumpkins are usually harvested after frost has killed the vines. Cut the fruit from the vine, leaving a few inches of stem attached. Wipe carefully with a cloth and place in a cool, dry location to cure. Stored in a warm, dry spot, the fruits will keep several months without further attention.

Pumpkin blossoms are also edible, and are best picked on sunny mornings after they fully open and morning dew has dried.

Radish *(Raphanus sativus)*

SEASON	Cool
DEGREE OF DIFFICULTY	Easy
CROP ROTATION GROUP	Roots Group
FERTILIZER	Balanced
CONTAINER GARDEN	Yes
DAYS TO HARVEST	25-40
INTERPLANTABLE	Yes

Radishes mature in less than a month, and are a great crop to introduce kids to vegetable gardening. Plant small amounts frequently as long as the weather remains cool. Salad radishes produce round roots or elongated ones, in red, white, purple, pink, and bicolors.

Despite their overall similarity, different varieties of radish will perform differently under the same garden conditions. Therefore, it is wise to experiment with several types to find one or two that give good results where you reside.

Do not confuse salad radishes with winter radishes, discussed separately. The latter are grown in fall for storage and use during the colder months.

Planting

The radish bed should contain plenty of organic matter. Radishes do not need a lot of nitrogen, but like most root crops benefit from added potassium and phosphorus. Wood ashes are a good source of these nutrients, along with bone meal. Add these amendments to the growing bed in winter, to give them time to break down before early spring planting.

As soon as the soil can be worked in spring, sow 2 or 3 seeds $1/2$ inch (1.25 cm) deep, spacing clumps $1^1/_2$ inches (3.75 cm) apart each way. You only need to plant a dozen or two clumps each week. As soon as the seeds have germinated, thin to one plant in each spot. Succession plantings can be made all spring, until the weather warms up. Hot, dry weather results in strong flavored, tough roots.

Small size and rapid growth make radishes an ideal container crop. Pots larger than about 6 inches (15.25 cm) in diameter are most satisfactory. Take care that they do not dry out or the quality of your harvest will be poor. Use a standard soil-less potting mix, and feed with a balanced organic fertilizer. Combine fertilizer with the soil mix. Radishes must grow rapidly in order to be tender and mild-flavored. Their short development time means fewer opportunities to feed them with soluble fertilizer, hence the recommendation to enrich the growing mix.

The qualities that make radishes good for containers also make them ideal for interplanting with other crops. A classic method is to plant radishes and carrots together. By the time the radishes are mature, the carrots will be large enough to thin, and pulling the radishes does so automatically. You can also interplant radishes with lettuce, scallions, or peas.

Cultivation
Keep radishes free of weeds or the yield will be reduced. Because they mature so rapidly, typically four weeks or less after germination, don't bother with mulch. Radishes do not need rich soil, but they need plenty of moisture.

Harvesting
Harvest radishes at about an inch (2.5 cm) in diameter. Pull up the plants and carefully wash off the soil. To store, cut off the tops, leaving about half an inch (1.25 cm) of green, drop the radishes into a resealable plastic bag and keep in the refrigerator.

Radish, Winter (*Raphanus sativus* and *R. sativus longipinnata*)

SEASON
Fall only

DEGREE OF DIFFICULTY
Moderate

CROP ROTATION GROUP
Roots Group

FERTILIZER
Balanced

CONTAINER GARDEN
No

DAYS TO HARVEST
50-65

INTERPLANTABLE
No

Winter radishes are planted in late summer for winter harvest. They store well, but must be harvested before temperatures fall below 20°F (-7°C). Varieties include black-skinned and green-skinned rounded forms, and the elongated type known in Asian cuisine as *daikon*. One green-skinned type has pink flesh and is known as *watermelon radish*. Pure white daikon is the variety most often seen outside Asian markets.

Winter radishes get much larger than salad radishes, and consequently require more space. Because their roots are large, they also require deep, well-cultivated soil in order to produce a worthwhile crop. As a rule, therefore, they are better suited to gardens where space is not at a premium.

Winter radishes are not winter-hardy and therefore timing is an important factor in producing a crop. They must be grown during a period of cool, short days, but cannot tolerate freezing temperatures. Mild winter areas provide the most favorable conditions for reliable production.

Planting

Sow seeds about six weeks before the first frost, in rich, well-drained, sandy soil. Soil that has been amended with wood ashes or bone meal will give the best results. Avoid nitrogen-rich fertilizers, which will produce heavy foliage at the expense of root development. Daikon types require deep, loose soil to produce top-quality roots.

Cultivate to at least 2 feet (61 cm) deep, or build correspondingly deep raised beds if you intend on having choice specimens. Do not plant these varieties in spring, as they require short days in order to produce roots. Water well. As soon as seeds have germinated, thin plants to a spacing of 6 inches (15.25 cm) in each direction. Time plantings to avoid hot weather. Seedlings may simply die if they germinate before the weather cools down.

Cultivation

Keep radishes free of weeds or the yield will be reduced. Radishes do not need nitrogen-rich soil, but they need plenty of moisture, at least 1 inch (2.5 cm) per week. Cultivate carefully around the plants to avoid damaging feeder roots. Apply a mulch to maintain soil moisture and smother weeds. The plants are seldom bothered by pests.

Harvesting

Harvest storage radishes before the ground freezes. The large plants will require digging and often cannot be simply pulled from the soil. Wash soil off the roots carefully, so as not to damage the skin. Remove all but 2 inches (5 cm) of the tops and store in damp, cool conditions, where they will keep for two to three months. Watermelon radishes get as large as a baseball, while daikon radishes a foot (30 cm) long are not uncommon. Really enormous specimens have been produced by dedicated gardeners.

Winter radishes are generally eaten raw as a condiment, made into pickles, or added directly to stir-fried dishes.

Scallions and Bunching Onions
(Allium cepa and Allium fistulosum)

SEASON
All

DEGREE OF DIFFICULTY
Easy

CROP ROTATION GROUP
Roots Group

FERTILIZER
Balanced

CONTAINER GARDEN
Yes

DAYS TO HARVEST
60

INTERPLANTABLE
Yes

Scallions and bunching onions do not produce an enlarged bulb. They are always started from seed and typically are harvested when about $1/4$ to $1/2$ inch (6.5 to 12.75 mm) in diameter. True scallions will overwinter only in milder climates. Bunching onions are identical in appearance and use but are perennial even where winters are harsh.

Both scallions and bunching onions are excellent choices for container growing and for interplanting with other crops, such as lettuce, carrots, radishes and peas. You can also include either of these onions in ornamental plantings, where they will provide a vertical accent. Because their culinary uses are so many and varied, every kitchen garden should have at least a few of these onions.

Planting

Start seeds indoors in cell trays, three to six seeds per cell, beginning in late winter. Sow in succession for a continuous harvest through spring and then start more in July for fall transplanting. Scallions require about 60 days to maturity. Transplant whole plugs from cell trays without trimming, spacing them 4 inches (10 cm) apart each way.

Alternatively, sow seeds directly in the growing bed, spacing them four inches each way. Drop about six seeds in a spot, to produce a clump of onions at harvest time. Cover with $^1/_4$ inch (6.5 mm) of fine soil or vermiculite, and water well. Expect germination in about a week. The small seedlings are easily overwhelmed by weeds. Remove any weeds as soon as you notice them.

Do not plant scallions where you have grown other members of the onion family in recent years.

Bunching onions, being perennial, will continue growing right through the summer, even in areas with hot, humid weather. Entire plants can be harvested, or you can simply cut off the tops for the kitchen and allow new leaves to grow from the roots.

Cultivation

Keep scallions and bunching onions free of weeds all season. Feed with a balanced organic fertilizer at transplant time, and again about two weeks later. Irrigate if rainfall is less than 1 inch (2.5 cm) per week. Yellowing foliage indicates insufficient nitrogen, which should be immediately corrected with a fast acting liquid fertilizer, such as manure tea.

Scallions and bunching onions are generally pest- and disease-free. Crop diseases that affect storage onions seldom affect them.

Harvesting

Pull scallions or bunching onions as you need them. In the case of scallions, quality suffers in hot weather, so it is best use them before summer heats up. Bunching onions remain usable throughout the season, provided they are not subjected to drought. During cool weather, you can cut off the bottom 1 inch (2.5 cm) of each scallion plant with its roots, replant, and get a second harvest in about a month. Bunching onions may be transplanted in fall or spring to establish new clumps anywhere you want them. Neither of these onion varieties is prone to produce flowers. When they do appear, you can save seeds if you like.

Spinach _(Spinacea oleracea)_

SEASON
Cool

DEGREE OF DIFFICULTY
Moderate

CROP ROTATION GROUP
Leaves and
Flowers Group

FERTILIZER
Nitrogen

CONTAINER GARDEN
Yes

DAYS TO HARVEST
30-50

INTERPLANTABLE
Yes

Spinach is an ancient green that likes cold weather. Gardeners in hot-summer areas can grow it in spring and fall. Where summers remain cool, spinach grows all season long. Spinach offers numerous advantages over other leafy green crops. It is far more nutritious, ounce for ounce, than lettuce or mustards, and can be grown when the weather is too cold for either of these. Spinach can be harvested small and used as a salad green, or allowed to mature. Mature plants can be harvested a few leaves at a time or the entire crop can be picked and preserved for later use.

Spinach has shallow roots and thus adapts well to container cultivation. Select a container that will hold about 2 cubic feet (61 cubic centimeters) of growing medium. Ideally, this will be a shallow box about the size of a wooden wine crate. Sow spinach seeds directly on the growing medium, and thin them for salad as mentioned above.

Planting

Spinach does best in sandy soil with plenty of added nitrogen. Sprinkle a half cup of cottonseed meal over every 8 square feet (2.5 square meters) of growing space. As soon as the ground is workable in spring, sow small patches of spinach in succession every week. Thin the plants to 4 inches (10 cm) apart each way when they are 2 inches (5 cm) tall. Add the removed plants to salad.

Spinach can also be started indoors in cell trays, and transplanted to the garden. Sow 2 or 3 seeds in each cell and water well. Place the tray where it will receive indirect light at a temperature of about 60°F (16°C). Germination should occur within a week to ten days. As soon as true leaves appear, thin to a single plant per cell. Feed the seedlings every week with a balanced liquid fertilizer. When they are 4 inches (10 cm) tall, transplant them to the garden, spacing them about 6 inches (15.25 cm) apart each way. Plants that are coddled in this fashion can develop leaves the size of ping pong paddles.

Spinach can be replanted as a fall crop, at which time starting the seeds indoors is preferable, especially if cooler temperatures can thus be maintained. Spinach varieties intended for overwintering also exist. These are planted in late fall, in time to develop a rosette of four to six leaves before the first hard freeze. In this state, they will sit dormant until spring warmth returns, providing the earliest harvest as daffodils appear in flower beds.

Cultivation

Keep the spinach bed irrigated, unless you receive an inch (2.5 cm) of rain per week. Mulch around the plants to retain moisture and keep the soil cool. Keep the plants green and growing by feeding every two weeks with a liquid fertilizer, such as manure tea. Spinach has few pests. Slugs are the primary threat and can be thwarted by methods discussed earlier. Aphids may become a problem when spinach is exposed to hot, dry conditions.

Harvesting

Harvest the largest leaves individually from each plant as you need them. Each crop should produce several pickings. Eight or 10 square feet (2.5 to 3 square meters) should produce about a pound (.5 kg) of spinach at each picking. When the new leaves begin to have pointed, rather than rounded, tips, it is time to harvest the remaining crop. If you have an excess, spinach freezes well. Place the washed leaves in a large kettle without draining them. Place the kettle over medium heat and steam the spinach until it is wilted, about three minutes. Drain, rinse with cold water, drain again, and pack into freezer containers.

Spinach Substitutes for Warm Climates

(Basella rubra, Tetragonia expansa)

During warm weather, most greens will go to seed. Quality and flavor suffer, as the greens become bitter flavored. These two forms of "summer spinach" fill in for the standard type during hot weather. Neither is grown exactly like spinach, however.

Malabar spinach (*Basella rubra*) is an Asian native vine. It requires a trellis, and is a good choice to follow peas. The stems in one popular variety are beet-red, making the plant a good choice for interplanting with ornamentals.

Planting

Seed germinates best at 80°F (27°C) and requires ten days to two weeks. Start seeds indoors in pots about a month before transplanting, and move to the garden when the weather is warm. Space plants 1 foot (30.5 cm) apart. Cool temperatures and dry soil inhibit germination. The vines are vigorous and cannot be maintained for long in seedling-size containers. Expect the weather to be suitable about a month after the last spring frost.

Cultivation

If planted to follow peas, no fertilization is necessary. Plants should receive an inch (2.5 cm) of water per week. Where peas did not precede the spinach, side dress every three weeks with a balanced organic fertilizer.

Harvesting

You can begin harvesting two months after transplanting. The plants regrow even if severely cut back. They will self-sow and should not be allowed to produce seeds if you do not desire a repeat performance. The smaller leaves can be separated from the stems and used as a salad green or chop leaves and stems and steam or boil them.

SEASON Warm	**CONTAINER GARDEN** Yes
DEGREE OF DIFFICULTY Easy	**DAYS TO HARVEST** 60 (New Zealand) 70 (Malabar)
CROP ROTATION GROUP Leaves and Flowers Group	**INTERPLANTABLE** No
FERTILIZER Nitrogen	

New Zealand Spinach

From New Zealand, as one might expect, this plant is like spinach in many respects. It grows with a vining or trailing habit, however, and can be picked throughout the summer. If interplanted with taller plants, or if provided with a trellis, it may climb. It is thus an excellent choice for interplanting in gardens of limited space.

The plant was discovered in Australia by Captain Cook and has the distinction of being the first vegetable from that continent to be introduced to European tables. It was cultivated by Maori people centuries prior to Cook's arrival.

Planting

Soak the seeds overnight to soften the seed coat and hasten germination. Sow in groups of three, spacing them 12 inches (30.5 cm) apart in fertile, well-drained soil. Expect seedlings to emerge in two to three weeks.

Cultivation

New Zealand spinach tolerates drought, but does best with regular irrigation. Keep the growing bed irrigated, unless you receive an inch (2.5 cm) of rain per week. Mulch around the plants to retain moisture and discourage weeds. Keep the plants green and growing by feeding every two weeks with a liquid fertilizer, such as manure tea. New Zealand spinach has essentially no pests. Even slugs and snails leave it alone.

Harvesting

In about two months after thinning, the plants will be ready to harvest. The leaves are tougher than conventional spinach, and are generally used as cooked greens rather than salad. Like spinach, the plants contain oxalic acid. Drop the leaves in boiling water for one minute, drain, rinse and then proceed with any recipe calling for cooked spinach.

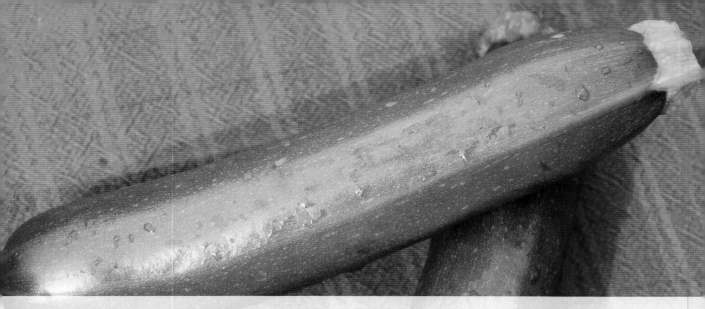

Squash, Summer *(Cucurbita pepo, C. moschata)*

Summer squash provides an abundant crop quickly and as a result is a favorite of backyard gardeners. Some varieties grow large, but plant breeders have developed compact forms that will fit into a raised bed garden or even a large tub. Summer squash types include straight- and crook-neck, pattypan, and zucchini. There is an unusual vining type shaped a bit like a trombone or trumpet. The color of the fruit ranges from bright golden yellow to deep green. Some varieties sport two colors.

Planting

Wait until the soil has warmed to 70°F (21°C) to plant the large seeds. Sow three seeds to a hill, spacing hills 2 to 3 feet (61 to 91.5 cm) apart each way. A 6-foot by 3-foot (183 by 91.5 cm) raised bed can accommodate two hills, for example. Place a tablespoon of balanced organic fertilizer in the planting hole. Firm the soil over the seeds, water well, and expect germination in about a week. When true leaves appear, thin to one plant per hill.

Cultivation

In general, follow the instructions given for cucumbers. Squashes are heavy feeders and respond to regular fertilization with amazing growth. Start feeding when the plants are about 1 foot (30.5 cm) tall and repeat every two weeks until blooms appear. Keep well watered. Water early in the day so leaves can dry in the sun before evening. This helps deter disease organisms.

Squashes fall victim to squash bugs, vine borers, and cucumber beetles. Keeping plants under row cover until blooms appear can thwart all these pests. Diseases are best controlled by following good cultural practices. Controlling insects also helps prevent the spread of disease. Specific advice on controlling the most common pests can be found in a previous section.

Harvesting

Male flowers will appear first, typically about six weeks after seedlings emerge. After a few days, female flowers, each with a baby squash below the petals, will appear. The flowers with the attached squash are considered a delicacy. Otherwise, wait until the flower drops and the fruit is about 6 to 8 inches (15.25 to 20.5 cm) in length. As a rule, smaller, younger fruits have the best flavor. Harvest all fruits before they mature to keep the plants producing.

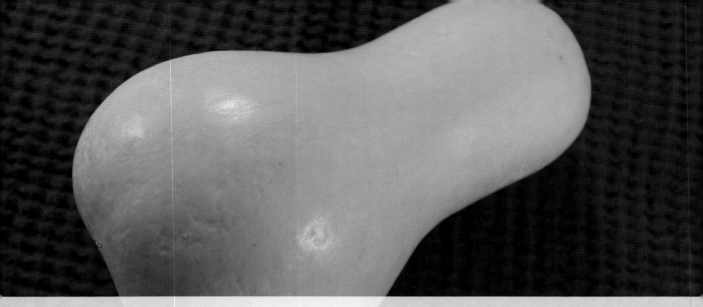

Squash, Winter *(Cucurbita argyrosperma, C. maxima, C. moschata, and C. pepo)*

Winter squashes keep well. They have thick, hard skins with yellow or orange flesh. Many grow large, but breeders have created compact forms suited to smaller-space gardens. Types include acorn, butternut, cushaws, and spaghetti squash. All grow with a vining habit and require a large, sturdy trellis if you do not have room to allow them to sprawl.

Acorn and butternut squashes are the most popular for culinary use. The cushaw types usually grow too large for home gardens and are used commercially to produce "pumpkin" pie filling. Spaghetti squash is an unusual type in which the cooked flesh resembles pasta and can be used in much the same way, paired with various sauces and condiments.

Squashes originated in the Andes and Mesoamerica and have been cultivated for so many centuries that the original connections to wild species have been lost. Botanists disagree as to the number of wild squashes, but it is somewhere between 10 and 35. Modern squash varieties are the result of extensive hybridization and selection that has been going on since pre-Columbian times.

Planting

Wait until the soil has warmed to 70°F (21°C) to plant the large seeds of winter squashes. Sow three seeds to a hill, spacing hills 2 to 3 feet (61 to 91.5 cm) apart each way. A 6-foot by 3-foot (183 by 91.5 cm) raised bed can accommodate two hills, for example. Place a tablespoon of balanced organic fertilizer in the planting hole. Firm the soil over the seeds, water well, and expect germination in about a week. When true leaves appear, thin to one plant per hill.

Install a sturdy trellis for each hill or arrange the hills in a row served by a single trellis. The trellis can be of any design you choose, but it must support the weight of the vines and a crop of 2 to 3 pound fruits.

Cultivation

Like summer squash, winter squashes are heavy feeders. Because they take longer to produce a crop, they will consume considerably more fertilizer. Side dress the plants every two weeks with a balanced organic fertilizer. Cease feeding when blooms appear.

If vine borers are a problem in your area, plant butternut types, which the borers avoid.

Mildew on the leaves of squashes can be controlled by spraying periodically with neem oil.

Harvesting

As fruits form, support them on the trellis with strips of cloth, tied to form a hammock. Each one can weigh 2 pounds (1 kg). When the skin becomes dull in appearance, press it with your fingernail. If the skin resists indentation, mark the calendar and harvest two weeks later. Leave 1 inch (2.5 cm) of stem attached to each fruit. Wipe off any soil with a towel. Do not wash. Winter squash keep best at a temperature of 45° to 50°F in a dry location. They should remain in good condition for four months.

Winter squash can be used in recipes as a substitute for pumpkin or sweet potatoes.

Tomatillo *(Physalis ixocarpa)*

SEASON
Warm

DEGREE OF DIFFICULTY
Easy

CROP ROTATION GROUP
Fruits Group

FERTILIZER
Balanced

CONTAINER GARDEN
Yes

DAYS TO HARVEST
65-90

INTERPLANTABLE
Yes

Tomatillos are little green "tomatoes" enclosed in a papery husk, which splits and curls back when the fruit is ripe. The tart, lemony flavor goes well in salsas and pickles. Plants bear abundantly but generally do not grow well in cool-summer areas or at higher latitudes than Washington, DC. Wait until the weather is warm and settled before putting transplants into the garden.

Like the tomato, tomatillos originated in Mexico. They have not caught on with the rest of the world in the same way that the tomato has, although both were brought back to Europe by the Spanish. Interestingly, the word *tomate,* which morphed into *tomato,* originally referred to the plant we know as a tomatillo. Gardeners with an interest in this plant should explore seed catalogs for heirloom varieties, of which many still exist in Mexico. Some produce fruits the color of eggplant, while others bear small, berry-like fruits of intense flavor. Plants range from knee-high to taller than a man.

Planting

Start seeds in cell trays at a temperature of 70°F (21°C) around the last frost date. Place 2 or 3 seeds in each cell, and thin to a single plant when true leaves appear. Snip the less vigorous seedlings off at the soil line. When the seedlings have two sets of true leaves, transplant to small pots. Keep watered and feed lightly with a balanced liquid fertilizer. It is important to keep the plants warm. Transplant to the garden, spacing plants 18 inches (45.75 cm) apart each way. Provide a tomato cage or a trellis to support the plants. Tomatillos will grow and bear fruit in poor, dry soil, but can produce an impressive harvest when conditions are less harsh.

Cultivation

While some cultivars will tolerate drought and heavy soils, tomatillos perform best in conditions similar to those preferred by tomatoes. Water new transplants daily for the first week. After that, water only if rainfall is less than 1 inch (2.5 cm) per week. Mulch helps keep the soil evenly moist and also prevents soil from splattering on the lower leaves, reducing the chances for fungal infections.

Tomatillos are ideal container plants. When grown in containers they should be supported with a stake sunk into the ground outside the container. Otherwise, the whole thing can tip over. Feed both in-ground and container-grown tomatillos every two weeks until blooms appear, using a balanced organic fertilizer.

Harvest

Fruits can be pulled from the plant and used when green or left to ripen, usually to a shade of golden yellow. Some varieties drop green fruit, others will hang on to the fruit until it is overripe. If you are unsure, pull fruits from the plant and store at room temperature without washing them. They will slowly ripen from green to yellow, and the flavor will change from sour to sweet. Tomatillos are rarely eaten raw. Drop them into simmering water for about eight minutes, drain, and cool before using. Many types of preserves can be made from tomatillos.

Tomato, Cherry *(Lycopersicum esculentum)*

For the beginning gardener, few crops are as rewarding as cherry tomatoes. With proper care a single plant will bear for several months, producing hundreds of delicious, bite-size fruits. Cherry tomatoes are probably most like the tomatoes originally domesticated in the Andes and first used as food in pre-Columbian Mexico. In tropical climates the plants are perennial.

Planting

For best results, select plants at your local garden center. Choose stocky, dark green plants about 6 to 8 inches (15.25 to 20.5 cm) tall. Wait until the soil temperature has reached 65°F (18°C) before transplanting them into the garden. To plant, remove all but the top one third of the leaves and bury the stem almost up to the lowermost set of remaining leaves. Add a tablespoon of balanced organic fertilizer to the planting hole. Unless the tomato variety is specifically recommended for small pots, use a 5-gallon (19-liter) container for each plant.

If you prefer to start your own tomato plants, begin up to two weeks before the last frost date in your area. The exact timing will depend upon your intentions. For the earliest tomatoes, you can plant almost any time after the frost date. However, if your goal is a trouble-free crop, it is wiser to wait for mild weather with nights generally above 60°F (16°C).

Sow seeds in cell trays, placing 2 or 3 seeds per cell. Water well and keep the trays at 70° to 75°F (21° to 24°C). Seedlings should appear in about one week. When the plants have true leaves, remove all but the strongest seedling by snipping the others off at soil level with scissors. When the seedlings have developed another set of leaves, transplant them to small pots, and begin feeding with a balanced organic fertilizer. You may also use a fertilizer formulated specifically for tomatoes. Some gardeners find these give excellent results. When the plants are large enough, move them to a permanent place in the garden.

Cultivation

Water new transplants daily for the first week. After that, water only if rainfall is less than 1 inch (2.5 cm) per week. Mulch helps keep the soil evenly moist and also prevents soil from splattering on the lower leaves, reducing the chances for fungal infections. Provide sturdy support via a tall stake, trellis, or tomato cage. Tomatoes grown in containers should be supported with a stake sunk into the ground outside the container. Otherwise, the whole thing can tip over. Feed in-ground and container-grown cherry tomatoes every two weeks until blooms appear, using a balanced organic fertilizer.

Harvesting

Days to maturity found on seed packets or in catalogs indicate the time from transplant to first harvest. The best harvest usually comes about two weeks later. For fresh eating, wait until the fruits are fully ripened and feel slightly soft when you squeeze them. Wipe fruits with a soft cloth and place them in an airy location at room temperature. Do not keep cherry tomatoes in your refrigerator, as temperatures below 50°F (10°C) will destroy the garden-fresh flavor.

Tomato, Determinate (Lycopersicum esculentum)

SEASON
Warm

DEGREE OF DIFFICULTY
Easy

CROP ROTATION GROUP
Fruits Group

FERTILIZER
Balanced

CONTAINER GARDEN
Yes

DAYS TO HARVEST
65-75

INTERPLANTABLE
Yes

Growing good tomatoes requires an understanding of their two growth forms—determinate and indeterminate. Determinate tomatoes reach a mature size and then bear most of their fruit all at once. They are typically compact plants good for small spaces but do not give a harvest over a long season.

Determinate tomatoes have been developed by plant breeders to serve the needs of commercial operations where uniformity of ripening and ease of harvest are the primary considerations, as opposed to flavor or nutritional value. Most determinate tomatoes are better when canned or made into sauce.

Planting

Purchase started plants at your local garden center and follow the planting instructions for cherry tomatoes.

If you prefer to start tomato plants from seeds, begin up to two weeks before the last frost date in your area. Sow seeds in a fine soil-less medium in cell trays, placing 2 or 3 seeds per cell. Water well and keep the trays at 70° to 75°F (21° to 24°C). Seedlings should appear in about one week. When the plants have true leaves, remove all but the strongest seedling by snipping the others off at soil level with scissors. When the seedlings have developed another set of leaves, transplant them to small pots, and

Determinate tomatoes bear heavily all at once.

begin feeding with a balanced organic fertilizer. You may also use a fertilizer formulated specifically for tomatoes. Some gardeners find these give excellent results. When the plants are large enough, move them to a permanent place in the garden.

Determinate tomato varieties lend themselves to support via wire cages, because the plants are short and bushy. Numerous designs for tomato supports exist. Suffice it to say that most of the commercially available ones are too short to be of value in warmer regions where even determinate tomatoes may reach the height of a grown man.

Cultivation

Tomatoes need nitrogen up until they begin blooming, but beyond that time added nitrogen will delay fruit production in favor of foliage growth. Many tomato problems are related to moisture control. Unless the plants show signs of wilting, do not irrigate. When you do water them, avoid getting the foliage wet. Determinate tomatoes are good candidates for container growing.

Tomatoes grown in containers should be surrounded with a wire cage and the cage secured to a ground stake. This prevents the whole thing from turning over in high winds.

Harvesting

Determinate tomatoes will bear most of their fruits in one large "flush," and are ideal for preserving. For canning, select red, ripe fruits that are still firm. Tomatoes can be frozen, too; just drop them in plastic bags and freeze. When thawed, the skins will slip off easily, and you can use the pulp in soups, stews, or spaghetti sauce.

Tomato, Heirloom *(Lycopersicum esculentum)*

SEASON
Warm

DEGREE OF DIFFICULTY
Moderate to Difficult

CROP ROTATION GROUP
Fruits Group

FERTILIZER
Balanced

CONTAINER GARDEN
Yes

DAYS TO HARVEST
70-90

INTERPLANTABLE
Yes

Heirloom tomatoes are typically varieties that have been saved by individuals, rather than the product of professional plant breeding. They come in a range of colors from almost white to almost black, with purple, green, yellow, orange, red, pink, and striped forms, and a range of sizes from that of a marble to over 2 pounds (907 g). Heirloom varieties, as a rule, are more difficult to grow than other types of tomatoes, but the exceptional flavors and range of colors tempt gardeners every season.

Planting

Follow the instructions for planting cherry tomatoes. Heirloom tomatoes may not be available as started plants, but you can start them indoors if you have a sunny window or suitable artificial light. Germinate seeds in cell trays at about 80°F (27°C) and then transplant to 3-inch (7.5 cm) pots when two sets of true leaves are present. Keep daytime temperatures at 80°F (27°C) and nights at 60°F (16°C) for best results. Gentle air movement supplied by an oscillating fan produces plants with sturdy stems. Water young plants sparingly. As with other types of tomatoes, wait until the soil temperature is 65°F (18°C) before transplanting.

Cultivation

Virtually all heirloom tomatoes are indeterminate in growth form. Indeterminate tomatoes do not stop growing. They must be supported and pruned in order to be maximally productive. However, they bear over a long season. Heirloom tomatoes may be subject to fungal diseases that more modern varieties resist. Different varieties have different degrees of resistance to disease.

Uneven watering causes fruit to split in hot weather. Poor irrigation habits can also lead to blossom end rot, a condition in which the fruit tip opposite the stem begins to turn brown and watery.

Use an 8-foot (2.5-meter) stake sunk at least 18 inches (45.75 cm) into the ground to support heirloom tomatoes, or a very large wire cage. Start tying the plant to the stake when the first blooms appear. Use strips of cloth or special soft twist ties to avoid damaging the stems.

To prune heirloom tomatoes, start by examining the point at which each leaf emerges from the main stalk. You should see a small side shoot, or sucker, beginning to grow from this spot. Completely remove all suckers up to the first bloom cluster. As the plant grows, continue tying it to the stake at intervals of about 1 foot (30.5 cm). Loop the tie around the stem just under a large leaf for maximum support. Suckers will appear at every leaf node. Remove all but the bottom pair of leaves from each sucker. Doing so prevents the sucker from taking energy that would otherwise go to fruit production, while maintaining good leaf cover that helps prevent the fruits from being damaged by hot sunshine. Suckering or pruning is not recommended where summers are hot, as the additional leaf cover prevents sun scald on the fruit.

Harvesting

Green tomatoes as hard as baseballs can be pan fried with or without breading. However, the chief attraction of heirloom tomatoes is their fine flavor, which is best appreciated when the fruits are fully colored and the flesh yields slightly to gentle pressure. Some varieties of heirloom tomatoes keep well at room temperature for weeks. Most, however, should be eaten on the day they are harvested.

Tomato, Hybrid *(Lycopersicum esculentum)*

SEASON
Warm

DEGREE OF DIFFICULTY
Easy

CROP ROTATION GROUP
Fruits Group

FERTILIZER
Balanced

CONTAINER GARDEN
Yes

DAYS TO HARVEST
65-90

INTERPLANTABLE
Yes

Hybrid tomatoes, which are widely available from garden centers, are easier to grow than heirlooms. Hybrids are produced by plant breeders via crossing two varieties to obtain plants with the desirable characteristics of both parents. Unfortunately for the home gardener, the seeds of hybrids are unlikely to produce plants like their parents. Most often, the various breeding lines that contributed to the hybrid parent sort themselves out in the next generation, resulting in a group of seedlings with varying characteristics. This is how new tomato varieties are sometimes created, but the project is not one for a limited space garden, as many seedlings must be grown to fruition and evaluated before the few "chosen ones" are identified.

Planting

Most garden centers feature several varieties of hybrid tomato plants. Examine the label and look for a series of letters after the name of the cultivar. The letters indicate resistance to diseases and pests. For example, the designation "VFN" means the variety is resistant to *Verticillium* and *Fusarium* wilts and to nematodes that attack the roots.

For best results, select stocky, dark green plants about 6 to 8 inches (15.25 to 20.5 cm) tall. Wait until the soil temperature has reached 65°F (18°C) before transplanting them into the garden. To plant, remove all but the top one third of the leaves and bury the stem almost up to the lowermost set of remaining leaves. Add a tablespoon of balanced organic fertilizer to the planting hole. Unless the tomato variety is specifically recommended for small pots, use a 5-five gallon (19-liter) container for each plant.

If you prefer to start tomato plants from seeds, begin up to two weeks before the last frost date in your area. Sow seeds in a fine soil-less medium in cell trays, placing 2 or 3 seeds per cell. Water well and keep the trays at 70° to 75°F (21° to 24°C). Seedlings should appear in about one week. When the plants have true leaves, remove all but the strongest seedling by snipping the others off at soil level with scissors. When the seedlings have developed another set of leaves, transplant them to small pots, and begin feeding with a balanced organic fertilizer. You may also use a fertilizer formulated specifically for tomatoes. Some gardeners find these give excellent results. When the plants are large enough, move them to a permanent place in the garden.

Cultivation

Hybrid tomatoes may be either determinate or indeterminate. Follow the previous recommendations for support, depending upon the type you select. Indeterminate forms need suckers removed where summers are mild. Suckers can be rooted in a container of water placed in a semi-shaded location. When they are well rooted, you can plant them for a late tomato crop.

Harvesting

Harvest hybrid tomatoes as you would the other varieties, choosing firm ripe fruits if preservation is your goal. For fresh eating, select fully ripened fruits that have an appetizing fragrance. Some hybrid varieties have been developed specifically for canning and making sauces. Others are suitable for drying. The vast majority are good for salads and sandwiches.

Tomato, Grafted _(Lycopersicum esculentum)_

SEASON
Warm

DEGREE OF DIFFICULTY
Easy

CROP ROTATION GROUP
Fruits Group

FERTILIZER
Balanced

CONTAINER GARDEN
Yes

DAYS TO HARVEST
70–90

INTERPLANTABLE
Yes

Tomatoes are among the most popular homegrown vegetables. As more people grow their own, interest in heirloom types has surged. Unfortunately, these delicious variations on the tomato theme can be difficult to grow because of disease susceptibility. In the last decade, grafted tomatoes have appeared on the retail market, and they offer a number of advantages to home gardeners.

Grafted tomatoes are created by hand, taking the root portion of a hardy and disease-resistant variety and grafting upon it the leafy portion of a delicious, but typically not very disease-resistant heirloom type. The resulting plant produces heirloom fruit on a modern resistant rootstock.

Grafting helps prevent leaf blights.

Planting

Grafted tomatoes cannot be produced directly from seed. You will need to purchase plants at a garden center or order them online. Grafting can be done at home, but it is not a project for the novice garden enthusiast. Transplant grafted tomatoes as described previously for other varieties. However, it is important not to bury the plants too deeply. If the graft scar is buried, the top growth will root from the stem above the scar, and all the benefits of grafting will be lost.

Cultivation

Grafted tomatoes grow just like other tomatoes, and are subject to problems related to improper watering. Likewise, they will not bear well if fertilization continues past the blooming stage. The majority of grafted tomatoes are indeterminate, and should have sturdy support. Apply mulch to keep the soil evenly moist.

Harvesting

Follow the recommendations given for other types of tomatoes. Grafted tomatoes may bear abundantly.

Turnips *(Brassica rapa var. rapifera)*

SEASON
Cool

DEGREE OF DIFFICULTY
Easy

CROP ROTATION GROUP
Roots Group

FERTILIZER
Balanced

CONTAINER GARDEN
Yes

DAYS TO HARVEST
40-80 days

INTERPLANTABLE
Yes

Turnips are an underappreciated vegetable. They are nutritious, easy to grow, and provide a crop when not much else is growing. If you don't like cooked turnips, try them raw, in coleslaw for example. Some turnips have purple shoulders on white roots, while others produce a pure white crop. Some cultivars are intended for production of greens only and are best for container growing.

Planting

Turnips should mature during cool weather. In warmer climate areas, choose a fast maturing variety for spring planting. Well-drained soil that is loose and crumbly will give the best results. Sow seeds about $^1/_4$ inch (6.35 mm) deep, water well, and thin seedlings to stand 4 inches (10 cm) apart each way.

Cultivation

If flea beetles are a problem, cover the bed with a floating row cover. Turnips do not require particularly fertile soil but need adequate moisture. Irrigate if rainfall is less than 1 inch (2.5 cm) per week. Water stress may bring on an attack of aphids.

Harvesting

After thinning, you can use the smaller plants as cooked greens or in salad. Harvest the roots when they reach the size you desire. Those smaller than 2 inches (5 cm) in diameter have the best flavor. Wash off the soil, cut the tops within 1 inch (2.5 cm) of the shoulder, and store in a plastic bag in the refrigerator where they will keep for weeks.

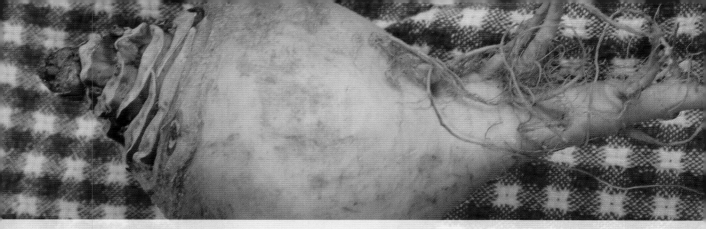

Rutabaga *(Brassica napus var. napobrassica)*

Rutabaga is best cultivated as a fall crop. The plants produce a globular root, like a turnip, with yellow-orange flesh and a distinctive flavor. While never the star of a TV cooking show, rutabaga can be used in hearty stews or other dishes where the sweet-earthy flavor of root vegetables can shine.

Planting

Sow seeds $^1/_4$ inch (6.35 mm) deep two months before the first frost, spacing about 2 inches (5 cm) apart. Cover with fine soil, firm gently and water well. Prior to the end of the first month of growth, thin to 8 inches (20.5 cm) apart. If thinned too late, roots will not develop properly. The plants can get bushy, and will produce roots the size of a softball or larger. They require ample room for proper development.

Cultivation

Culture is the same as for turnips, although rutabaga requires about 90 days to mature.

Harvesting

Rutabaga greens are not often mentioned, but they are edible. You can steal a few smaller, leaves from each plant and add them directly to a salad, or steam them like spinach. Don't remove too many leaves from a plant or root growth will be impeded. Harvest when the roots are about 4 inches (10 cm) across. Harvest before the first hard freeze. Cure a few days in a cool, dry place then brush off the soil and store in cool, damp conditions.

SEASON
Fall

DEGREE OF DIFFICULTY
Moderate

CROP ROTATION GROUP
Roots Group

FERTILIZER
Balanced

CONTAINER GARDEN
No

DAYS TO HARVEST
90

INTERPLANTABLE
No

Watercress *(Nasturtium officinale)*

SEASON
Cool

DEGREE OF DIFFICULTY
Easy

CROP ROTATION GROUP
Leaves and
Flowers Group

FERTILIZER
Nitrogen

CONTAINER GARDEN
Yes

DAYS TO HARVEST
45

INTERPLANTABLE
No

Watercress has been consumed since ancient times and is naturalized in many parts of the world.

Planting

Watercress need not be grown in running water; it adapts well to container culture. Hardy to Zone 4, it can be started from seed or cuttings. The latter can be rooted in a glass of water, and transplanted when the roots are 2 inches (5 cm) in length. Watercress needs clean, slightly alkaline water and will not thrive if planted in acidic conditions or in water that is stagnant. Use a mix of sand, gravel, and a small amount of compost. Avoid peat- and pine-based components. Thoroughly water the mix before planting. Mulch the surface with pea gravel to keep the compost from floating out of the pot. Scatter seeds thinly on the surface of the gravel, or poke rooted cuttings into the mix with your finger.

Cultivation

Keep the plants well watered. This may mean multiple daily waterings during hot weather. In addition, the plants will need regular fertilization due to the frequent watering. Grow watercress in full sun with afternoon shade during hot weather.

Harvesting

Watercress is ready to harvest about two months after sowing seeds, sooner if started from cuttings. Each plant will yield multiple pickings. In mild-winter areas watercress is evergreen, and can be lightly harvested all winter. The plants are hardy to USDA Zone 4.

Upland Cress (*Barbarea verna*)

Upland cress, also called creasy greens, land cress, and several other names, is native to Europe. It has been cultivated at least since the seventeenth century and was no doubt foraged by ancient people. It requires far less moisture than watercress, and therefore is less trouble to grow. Because it grows quickly from seed and seldom grows taller than 8 inches (20.5 cm) upland cress is an ideal container garden plant.

Planting
Grow upland cress with other green crops in raised beds or containers in a gritty, neutral mix amended with compost and a nitrogen source. Direct-seed in early spring or late summer. Successive plantings may be made as long as the plants can mature in cool weather. Heat produces rangy growth and harsh flavors.

Cultivation
Keep the bed well watered and free of weeds. Additional feeding is not necessary. Plants growing in containers should be fed with soluble fertilizer at every third or fourth watering. It is important, for the best quality greens, to keep the plants growing steadily and without stress.

Harvesting
Upland cress will be ready for harvest in about six weeks from germination. Cut the leaves at soil level. If the plants are in containers, compost the root mass.

SEASON
Cool

DEGREE OF DIFFICULTY
Easy

CROP ROTATION GROUP
Leaves and
Flowers Group

FERTILIZER
Nitrogen

CONTAINER GARDEN
Yes

DAYS TO HARVEST
50

INTERPLANTABLE
Yes

Perennial Crops

Perennial plants are those that return year after year, with or without the assistance of the gardener. Perennial crops include vegetables, numerous herbs and seasonings, and small fruits that can be accommodated in a backyard space.

Perennial herbs are discussed in a separate section that follows. This section covers the others.

Among the most useful of perennial crops are the various types of onions. Gardeners with sufficient space should consider devoting separate beds to the production of garlic, shallots, and storage onions, with the size of those beds determined by kitchen needs. The plants are among the most productive you can grow.

Globe artichokes are a delicacy that will not grow easily everywhere, but the quality and flavor of a well-grown crop is superior to anything available in the marketplace.

Small fruits, such as blueberries, blackberries, raspberries, and strawberries, can be tucked into the corners of the garden, especially if you use more recently developed compact varieties. Because these fruits are highly perishable after picking, the quality of homegrown ones almost always beats the market. The main drawback is that fruits require a bit more attention in terms of annual maintenance than other perennial crops.

Among the most valuable edible perennials are Jerusalem artichokes, asparagus, horseradish, and rhubarb. Properly planted and maintained, these crops will bear a harvest year after year without replanting or relocation. Rhubarb and Jerusalem artichokes are also decorative and can be used as a garden accent. However, if only one perennial patch can be accommodated, choose asparagus. A single planting will provide harvests long after the gardener has departed, providing pleasure each spring for generations.

Because perennials may take a season or two before harvest can begin, novice gardeners are encouraged to include these plants in their garden plans from the beginning. Other than globe artichokes, none of them are a challenge to grow in much of the world.

Artichoke, Globe *(Cynara scolymus)*

SEASON Perennial	The globe artichoke is a giant thistle, the edible part of which is the unopened flower bud. Until recently, all globe artichokes were considered perennial vegetables and could be successfully grown only where their narrow cultural requirement could be met. This was because in the older varieties, two years were required to obtain mature plants from seed. Recent breeding success has produced a variety that matures a crop in only one season, giving hope to growers unable to bring the standard varieties through winter. This variety can be grown in a large container, such as half a whiskey barrel, or you can create a separate bed, about 3 feet (1 m) square, to accommodate one plant.

SEASON
Perennial

DEGREE OF DIFFICULTY
Difficult

CROP ROTATION GROUP
None

FERTILIZER
Balanced

CONTAINER GARDEN
Yes

DAYS TO HARVEST
90–120

INTERPLANTABLE
No

The globe artichoke is a giant thistle, the edible part of which is the unopened flower bud. Until recently, all globe artichokes were considered perennial vegetables and could be successfully grown only where their narrow cultural requirement could be met. This was because in the older varieties, two years were required to obtain mature plants from seed. Recent breeding success has produced a variety that matures a crop in only one season, giving hope to growers unable to bring the standard varieties through winter. This variety can be grown in a large container, such as half a whiskey barrel, or you can create a separate bed, about 3 feet (1 m) square, to accommodate one plant.

Planting

If your climate is moderate during the summer months and experiences only light frosts in winter, you can give perennial artichokes a try with a reasonable expectation of success. Otherwise, seek out the annual form.

Sow seeds ¹⁄₄ inch (6.35 mm) deep two months before the last expected frost, in 4-inch (10-cm) pots maintained at 75°F (24°C). When the seedlings have four true leaves, transplant to 6-inch (15.25-cm) pots. Keep them in bright light at around

65°F (18°C) during the day, with a 10°F (5°C) temperature drop at night. They are ready when they are two months old provided the soil has warmed to 60°F (16°C) or more. Move them to organically rich, moisture-retentive soil, and sprinkle $\frac{1}{4}$ cup (59 ml) of cottonseed meal into the planting hole.

If your seedlings are ready before the soil outside is warm enough, simply transplant them to a larger container. Avoid letting them become root bound, or they may be set back when they arrive at their final destination.

Cultivation

Make sure artichokes receive ample water. Irrigate if rainfall is less than 1 inch (2.5 cm) per week. In about three months from transplant, the annual type will bear its first flowers. Other varieties won't mature until the following spring. Where the potential for winter freezing exists, cover the plants with a large basket, piling leaves on top for additional insulation to protect them from the cold. This should be done after leaves naturally die back at the end of the season.

One of the chief issues in over-wintering an artichoke is preventing crown rot. Covering too densely or using a moisture-retentive mulch may kill the plant. Hence the recommendation for a basket, to create an area of relatively dry air around the crown. The colder the winter, the deeper the mulch on top of the basket will need to be.

Harvesting

The primary flower bud forms at the top of a thick stalk emerging from the rosette of leaves. Removing it stimulates the formation of additional buds on side shoots, although none will be as large as the first bud. Harvest each bud, primary or secondary, while it remains tight, showing no sign of opening. Cut the stem about 4 inches (10 cm) below the base of the bud. Place the stem in water and refrigerate. Use promptly, within a week or less. Freezing and pickling are the best preservation methods.

Artichoke, Jerusalem *(Helianthus tuberosus)*

SEASON
Perennial

DEGREE OF DIFFICULTY
Easy

CROP ROTATION GROUP
None

FERTILIZER
Balanced

CONTAINER GARDEN
Yes

DAYS TO HARVEST
Approximately 180

INTERPLANTABLE
No

Jerusalem artichoke is neither an artichoke nor from Jerusalem. Rather, it is a native North American sunflower that was introduced to Europeans by indigenous Americans. It is thought that *Jerusalem* is a distortion of the Italian word for sunflower, *girasole*. As for the *artichoke* part, that is attributed to the French explorer Samuel de Champlain, who sent the first examples to France with a comment that the flavor resembled that of artichokes. With that sweet-nutty flavor and a potato-like texture, the tubers are produced in large quantities, making this a great crop for small space gardens.

Jerusalem artichokes are easy to establish in a sunny corner of the garden. However, they can become a weed if not properly managed. To prevent self-sowing, the plants must be harvested before flower open. Dig all the tubers in the patch each season, saving some for replanting and using the rest in the kitchen. This not only prevents unwanted plants from popping up, but allows you to renew the soil over the winter by adding organic amendments. If replanted again and again in old soil, productivity is reduced, and worse, the kitchen quality suffers.

You can also plant Jerusalem artichokes in a large container. This makes harvesting a cinch, as you merely dump the growing mix and separate out the tubers. Doing so also avoids leaving a stray tuber behind to cause problems later. Choose as large a container as you can manage. A single tuber the size of your thumb can produce 100 offspring by season's end.

Planting

Plant dormant tubers in early spring in well-drained garden soil, covering them to a depth of 1 inch (2.5 cm). Soil of average fertility will give good results. Avoid heavy clay soils, opting instead for loose, sandy loam with plenty of organic matter. Space the tubers about 12 inches (30.5 cm) apart each way, and keep the growing area free of weeds until the plants are up and growing. Once they have a foothold, the artichokes will crowd out any weed seedlings.

For container production, choose any good commercial potting mix and combine it with a balanced organic fertilizer according to the manufacturer's directions.

Cultivation

The Jerusalem artichoke needs little care. Fertilization is not required during the growing season, and the plants are reasonably drought-tolerant. They will, however, need irrigation in arid regions. Mulch applied around the base of the plants will help keep the soil moist and cool and its decomposition will supply nutrients. Each year after spring planting, sprinkle a tablespoon or two of balanced organic fertilizer around the emerging plants.

Plants grown in containers will need more frequent watering and fertilization. A soluble fertilizer applied about every fourth watering should be sufficient.

Harvesting

Dig tubers before blooms appear, about three to four months after shoots emerge. Dig the entire patch, unless you want plants to establish themselves. To prevent unwanted spreading, replant stored tubers each spring. Store the tubers as described for potatoes. Jerusalem artichokes are eaten boiled, mashed, or fried, like potatoes.

Asparagus *(Asparagus officinalis)*

SEASON
Perennial

DEGREE OF DIFFICULTY
Moderate

CROP ROTATION GROUP
None

FERTILIZER
Balanced

CONTAINER GARDEN
No

DAYS TO HARVEST
One year

INTERPLANTABLE
No

The word *asparagus* is Latin and meant to the ancients what it means to us today. It is depicted in ancient Egyptian art and mentioned in the earliest known cookbook. This delectable vegetable is a member of the lily family. Two seasons of growth are required to get an asparagus patch producing. Once established, however, the asparagus bed will continue to yield a harvest each spring for decades.

Asparagus has not been the subject of much selective breeding until modern times. New strains have been introduced as recently as 2011. Part of the reason may be that a well-maintained bed of asparagus can remain productive for years without replanting. Therefore, little incentive exists for replacing existing plants with newer varieties.

Planting

In fall before planting, check the soil pH with a test kit and add lime to adjust the pH to neutral. Check again in spring, adding additional lime if the test shows an acidic pH (below 7). Purchase plants from a reputable source. This not only reduces the wait from three years to two, but also avoids dealing with the delicate, fussy seedlings. Choose an "all-male" variety. Male asparagus plants out-produce females by three to one. Also, seedlings dropped from female plants can become weeds.

Store dormant plants in a cool, dry place and wait until the soil temperature has reached 50°F before planting. Set plants about 6 inches (15.25 cm) deep, adding a tablespoon of bone meal to each planting hole. Space the plants 18 inches (45.75 cm) or more apart each way, and spread the roots out on the bottom of the hole. Do not compact the soil.

Cultivation

Mulch the asparagus bed with 2 inches (5 cm) of leaves, straw, or compost. Remove any weeds that come up through the mulch. Asparagus resents competition and weeds reduce yield. Irrigate during dry spells, but do not allow water to stand around the plants.

Asparagus is relatively salt tolerant. Sprinkling a small amount of salt on the asparagus bed will suppress weeds without harming the asparagus. Use about a tablespoon (15 gm) of salt per 25 square feet (2.32 square meters).

The only major pest is the asparagus beetle. It can be deterred by planting tomatoes near the asparagus patch, and by spraying the plants with neem oil.

Harvesting

Do not harvest during the first season after transplanting. During the second season, take only one or two shoots from each plant. In subsequent years, you can harvest more heavily. After harvest, side-dress the plants with compost, and give each one a tablespoon of balanced organic fertilizer. Once established, each plant should produce $^1/_2$ pound (227 g) of asparagus per season.

Asparagus is best eaten fresh but can be frozen or pickled. Asparagus can be boiled, steamed, grilled, or quickly fried, baked in quiches and casseroles, and enjoyed raw. The Roman Emperor Augustus coined the phrase "faster than cooking asparagus" when he expected quick results from his minions.

Blueberry (*Vaccinium corymbosum, V. virgatum, V. angustifolium*, and hybrids)

SEASON
Perennial

DEGREE OF DIFFICULTY
Moderate

CROP ROTATION GROUP
None

FERTILIZER
Acidic formula

CONTAINER GARDEN
Yes

DAYS TO HARVEST
2 years

INTERPLANTABLE
No

Blueberries are perennial shrubs native to North America. Wild ones, which can still be harvested in numerous locations along the Appalachian mountain chain, are sometimes called "huckleberries." Blueberries were not cultivated in Europe until the twentieth century.

Three types of blueberries are available, each adapted to different temperature regimes. High-bush blueberries can reach 6 feet (1.8 m) in height and are adapted to cooler climates. Hybridization has produced plants that are more heat-tolerant. Low-bush blueberries are about half the size of their tall cousins and more heat-tolerant but otherwise similar. The third variety, rabbiteye blueberries, are suited to warm climates. Recent plant breeding has resulted in compact blueberry cultivars that adapt well to container growing or small-space gardens. These newer varieties tend to be more adaptable in terms of temperature as well.

Although high-bush blueberries are remarkably productive, they require the longest time to reach full production, and require careful pruning. The more compact forms are better suited to small space gardens in most of the temperate zone.

Planting

Blueberries require acid soil, at a pH of 5.5 or below. You therefore should prepare special beds for blueberries, keeping them well supplied with acidic components like pine needles and peat moss. Growing in containers facilitates providing the correct pH without affecting adjacent plants. Five gallons (19 L) is an appropriate container size for a single plant. Blueberries also need full sun and good drainage. Wet soil will result in root rot.

Purchase container-grown plants of known cultivars and transplant to the garden in late winter while plants remain dormant. Keep plants well watered to help establish a healthy root system but do not overdo it.

It is wise to purchase at least two blueberry plants. Cross-pollination, though not always required, will always increase fruit production.

Cultivation

Remove and discard all flowers during the first season. If plants are sold in fruit, remove and discard the berries. Eliminating flowers and fruit forces the plant to put energy into root production. Pruning is the key to maintaining health and, in turn, productivity. If you grow high-bush blueberries, prune away all five-year-old canes annually. Low-bush blueberry types, on the other hand, fruit best on canes produced directly from the roots, rather than from buds on above-ground wood. Pruning is therefore done to encourage the former at the expense of the latter, by removing older canes all the way to the base. Pruning should be done while the plants are dormant.

Harvesting

Harvest blueberries as they ripen. It may be necessary to use netting to protect the crop from marauding birds. If space permits, choosing a selection of cultivars will result in harvest over most of the summer season.

Blueberries are most often made into desserts or preserved as jam, but their combination of sweetness and acidity makes them suitable for savory dishes as well.

Garlic *(Allium sativum var. sativum)*

SEASON
Overwinter

DEGREE OF DIFFICULTY
Easy

CROP ROTATION GROUP
Roots Group

FERTILIZER
Balanced

CONTAINER GARDEN
Yes

DAYS TO HARVEST
Approximately 200

INTERPLANTABLE
No

Every cuisine seems to include dishes that feature the distinct, savory flavor of garlic. Through centuries of cultivation, garlic varieties have adapted to nearly every place on Earth habitable by humans, although its earliest use was in Asia roughly 7000 years ago. Garlic quickly forms "landraces," varieties well-adapted to a particular growing locale. Check with your local garden center or online to choose a variety best adapted to your part of the country.

The many cultivated forms of garlic may be divided into two groups, hard-necked and soft-necked forms. Hard-necked garlic, also known as *rocambole,* is typically grown in cooler climates, while soft-necked types favor warmer weather.

Garlic can be grown in a container, although this is not the ideal way if you are interested in productivity. It can also be easily tucked in among ornamental plantings.

Freshly pulled garlic should be spread out to cure for a few days.

Planting

Plant garlic in rich, moist, well-drained soil and keep the patch free of weeds. Set individual cloves about 4 inches (10 cm) apart, pressing them gently into the soil until the tips are about $1/4$ inch (6.35 mm) below the surface. Do not remove the papery skin from the cloves. It helps protect against rot. The best time to plant garlic is in late summer or early fall. The plants will grow over the winter and should be ready to harvest the following summer.

Cultivation

When new foliage begins to emerge from the garlic plants, side dress them with a balanced organic fertilizer. Keep the growing area scrupulously free of weeds, as their presence can negatively impact productivity. Irrigate if rainfall does not provide adequate moisture.

Should flower scapes, or stalks, appear, cut them off near the point where they emerge from the leaves. The scapes are delicious when stir fried, and can be eaten raw in salad. Removing them forces the plant's energy into bulb production.

Harvesting

Baby garlic can be pulled any time after the shoots appear in spring. You can plant cloves at a 2-inch (5 cm) spacing and then thin out every other one if you want a crop of baby garlic. Pull all the babies before the plants are more than 1 foot (30.5 cm) tall. This will result in the largest bulbs for the remaining plants.

A pound of starter bulbs will yield anywhere from 3 pounds (1.35 kg) to more than 10 pounds (4.5 kg) of bulbs, depending on the variety and cultural conditions. Garlic is mature when the leaves begin to turn yellow. Pull the entire plant. Allow to dry thoroughly in a shady, well-ventilated spot for a day or two, and then gently rub off the dirt, taking care to leave the cloves well protected by their papery skins.

Allow the bulbs to cure in a warm, airy place, arranging them so they are not touching. After two weeks braid the garlic stems, or trim off all but 1 inch (2.5 cm) of stem and store in a warm, dry, dark place. To prevent weevils from attacking stored garlic, place the bulbs in the freezer for an hour before storing them. This will kill any insect eggs that may be present in the bulbs.

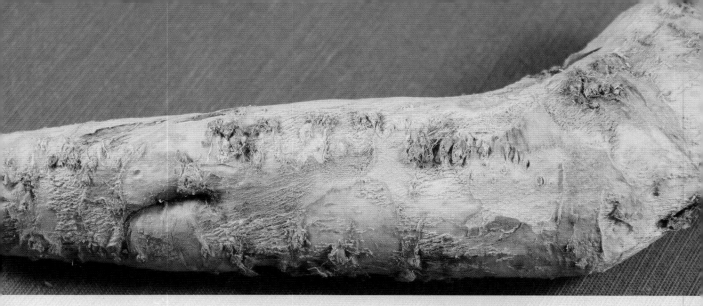

Horseradish *(Amoracia rusticana)*

SEASON
Perennial

DEGREE OF DIFFICULTY
Easy

CROP ROTATION GROUP
None

FERTILIZER
None

CONTAINER GARDEN
Yes

DAYS TO HARVEST
Approximately 250

INTERPLANTABLE
No

Known since antiquity, horseradish probably originated in eastern Europe or western Asia. It is hardy in USDA Zones 2 through 9, and has been naturalized in many parts of the world. Horseradish is a member of the mustard family and has a huge white taproot with foliage resembling turnip tops. It adds a special heat to many kinds of sandwiches and dishes.

Horseradish heat is the plant's way of protecting itself from root-munching herbivores. Undamaged, the root has no apparent aroma. But when cut or grated, the damaged cells release enzymes that produce mustard oil, which is responsible for the distinctive "bite" in the sweet, earthy flavor.

Planting
Horseradish is extremely easy to grow in any well-drained soil of average fertility. Plant a piece of root in a corner of the garden in full sun in late winter or early spring, before growth begins. As the weather warms in spring, the root will sprout and establish itself.

Because of its invasive tendencies, horseradish is a good candidate for cultivation in a large container. Amend the potting mix with a small amount of balanced organic fertilizer at planting time. Renew the potting mix annually after you harvest the roots.

Despite the name, horseradish is dangerous for horses.

Cultivation

Water the plant during dry spells, but otherwise leave it alone. Do not fertilize, which may lead to rampant, weedy growth. This includes container plants, which should only be fed if the leaves begin to show yellowing. Horseradish is legendary for its tenacity. Once established, the plants will continue to grow in the same spot for decades. Harvesting at the proper time prevents the plants from flowering and self-seeding. If flower spikes form, cut the entire plant off at ground level. This will do no harm, and the plant will return the following spring.

Expect the foliage to reach 3 feet (.9 m) in height. Small, tender leaves can be removed and chopped to add a mild horseradish flavor to dressings or sauces.

Harvesting

Where winters are bitter, do not harvest during the first year. After the first winter has passed, dig up the root in early spring and replant a portion. Allow the plant to grow for a year, and dig again in spring. Where winters are not harsh and the growing season is long, spring-planted horseradish can be harvested the following autumn. Wait until frost kills the foliage, then dig the roots, replanting a portion for next year. Once the plants are established, you can repeat this indefinitely.

Shredded or grated horseradish is used as a condiment or seasoning. The enzymatic reaction that produces the flavoring agents will begin to break down when the root is exposed to air. The snowy white flesh will darken, and the flavor will change from sharp to bitter. To prevent this, place shredded horseradish in a nonreactive container and add vinegar to cover. It will keep in the refrigerator for several months.

Some gardeners prefer to confine horseradish to a container.

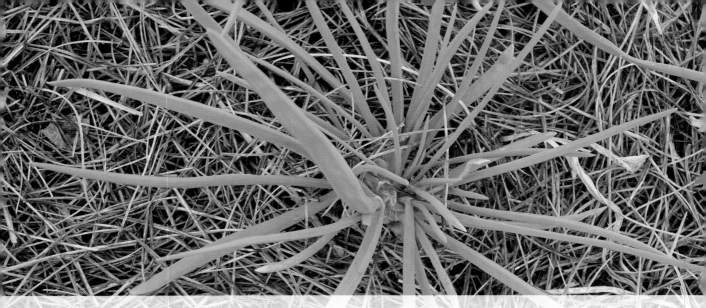

Perennial Onions *(Allium cepa var. aggregatum, A. cepa var. proliferum* and *Allium ampeloprasum)*

SEASON
Perennial

DEGREE OF DIFFICULTY
Easy

CROP ROTATION GROUP
Roots Group

FERTILIZER
Balanced

CONTAINER GARDEN
Not recommended

DAYS TO HARVEST
Approximately 250

INTERPLANTABLE
No

Perennial onions should receive more attention from home gardeners. Once a bed is established, they will deliver a crop for years with minimal care. There are several types of perennial onions.

The "mother," "multiplier," or "potato" onion divides during the growing season to produce several more. Replant without harvesting for a couple of seasons to establish a patch. Thereafter, use bulbs larger than 2 inches (5 cm) for the kitchen and replant the rest.

Egyptian or walking onions are grown for their foliage and are used like scallions. They produce little bulbs where you'd otherwise expect flowers. When the bulbs are large enough, the stalk bends over, and they plant themselves a short distance from the parent. In this manner, they "walk."

A third possibility is the perennial leek. It dies back in summer and resprouts in early fall. The sprouts can be harvested from winter through spring, when they will yield greens early in the season and baby leeks later on. Save some to keep the patch going.

Bunching onions are perennial scallions and were discussed in a previous section. They form clumps as just described for perennial leeks.

Planting

All perennial onions produce well and will grow in all parts of the continental United States. Plant them in rich, sandy soil amended with compost, bone meal, and wood ashes. Set plants or bulbs about 4 inches (10 cm) apart.

Cultivation

Keep the bed weeded, but be careful, as the roots are shallow and easily damaged. Mulch helps suppress weeds and keep soil moisture even, which onions prefer.

Harvesting

Perennial onions may not produce well during the first year as they are becoming established. Thereafter, they should yield well every year. This crop can produce a larger yield per square foot than any other crop except tomatoes. You can harvest green tops at any time after they appear, but wait until late summer or early autumn to harvest bulbs. Store potato onions like regular storage onions. Harvest perennial leeks, walking onions, and bunching onions at the size you desire for cooking. Otherwise, leave them in the ground.

Raspberries and Blackberries *(Rubus sp.)*

SEASON Perennial	

SEASON
Perennial

DEGREE OF DIFFICULTY
Moderate

CROP ROTATION GROUP
None

FERTILIZER
Balanced

CONTAINER GARDEN
Yes

DAYS TO HARVEST
1 year

INTERPLANTABLE
No

Blackberries and raspberries grow as multistemmed small shrubs. Individual stems, called *canes,* are often studded with thorns, although thornless cultivars have been developed. Numerous other varieties have been produced via selection and hybridization.

Plant breeding has resulted in raspberry cultivars suitable for container culture. Other than these types, both blackberries and raspberries should be grown in beds.

Planting

Both raspberries and blackberries require one season of growth before producing a crop the second year. They fruit on new growth borne on one-year-old canes. After fruiting, the canes die and should be pruned off.

Trellising, although not necessary, will improve productivity, reduce the likelihood of disease, and make fruit easier to pick. By keeping the canes separated, old canes can be easily removed after fruiting. This allows the plant to put more energy into next year's crop, rather than maintaining the now-useless fruited canes.

All bramble fruits require full sun and a deep, well-drained soil of average fertility and high organic matter content. Lay out a patch about 3 feet (91.5 cm) wide, allowing 5 feet (152.5 cm) of length for each plant. Remove sod, work the soil to a depth of 1 foot (30.5 cm), and incorporate at least 2 inches (5 cm) of organic matter.

Next, install the trellis. This can be a simple wire fence, a double fence, or a T-bar arrangement about 4 to 5 feet (122 to 152.5 cm) tall.

Set plants 5 feet (152.5 cm) apart in early spring, before the plants have broken dormancy. Container-grown plants often appear in garden centers in mid- to late spring, the proper planting time for nondormant stock. After planting dormant stock, cut the canes back to 6 inches (15.25 cm) to stimulate new growth (container-grown plants need pruning only to remove dead or damaged portions). Apply 2 inches (5 cm) of any organic mulch to conserve moisture.

Cultivation, Pruning, and Harvesting Routine

Keep the bed free of weeds and provide 1 inch (2.5 cm) of water per week from the time green leaves appear until fruit forms. Cease irrigation when fruit is colored; watering at this stage will reduce quality. Follow these steps to keep plants producing, beginning in the second year.

Year 1: In late winter to early spring, remove dead or diseased canes from container-grown stock at planting time. Cut back dormant stock to 6 inches (15.25 cm).

In summer, separate canes and tie them to one side of the trellis.

In fall, remove any inferior canes and cut all canes 1 foot (30.5 cm) taller than the trellis. Wait to do this until after a couple of frosts.

Year 2: In late spring, last year's canes will flower and new canes will emerge. Tie new canes to the side of the trellis opposite last year's canes.

In summer, harvest fruit from last year's canes, allowing this year's canes to grow.

In fall, after a couple of frosts, remove all of last year's canes and cut this year's canes back to 1 foot (30.5 cm) taller than the trellis.

Repeat this pattern in subsequent years.

Rhubarb *(Rheum rhabarbarum)*

SEASON Perennial	**CONTAINER GARDEN** No
DEGREE OF DIFFICULTY Moderate	**DAYS TO HARVEST** 365
CROP ROTATION GROUP None	**INTERPLANTABLE** No
FERTILIZER Low nitrogen	

Rhubarb is an ancient plant whose genetic history is largely unknown. Used by the Chinese for millennia as a medicine, the plant spread westward to Russia and Europe and arrived in the United States with European immigrants.

Rhubarb is grown from root cuttings. Like asparagus, it requires establishment in rich, fertile, well-drained soil for a couple of seasons before you can begin to harvest the juicy stems.

The leaves and roots of rhubard are poisonous, and its culinary use is limited to the bright red stems. When young and tender they can be eaten with sugar as a snack, but more often rhubarb is cooked.

Planting

Purchase plants from your local garden center in fall or winter if possible. Spring planting is less reliable. Do not plant rhubarb where summer temperatures exceed 90°F. In warm, temperate climates, locate the rhubarb patch where it will receive afternoon shade during the hottest part of the year. Soil for rhubarb should be slightly acidic and amended with bone meal and greensand to supply phosphorus and potassium. Too much nitrogen is undesirable, however. Although drainage is important, excessively sandy soil is not suitable for rhubarb. Set plants about 3 feet (91.5 cm) apart in each direction.

Cultivation

Keep plants irrigated if rainfall is insufficient. Fertilize with a balanced organic fertilizer each spring as new shoots emerge. Keep the bed free of weeds. In warm-summer areas, it is normal to lose up to a quarter of the patch each season due to heat. If this happens, dig and divide the plants the following spring to renew the patch. Plant divisions as just described for purchased plants. Cut off the flower spikes as they appear, to prevent any potential for self-sowing. Rhubarb is thought to be a natural hybrid, and seedlings are unlikely to reflect the kitchen qualities of the parent.

Harvesting

Harvest the red stems by cutting them off at ground level, and trim off all the green, leafy portion. Take only one third of the stalks from any given plant at one time. You can harvest twice each week for two months if the plants are well established.

Harvest again in the fall, taking all the stalks from each plant. Do this before cold weather causes the plants to die back naturally.

The stalks are typically trimmed like celery, then cut into 1-inch (2.5-cm) pieces. Combine the pieces with sugar, using roughly half as much sugar by weight as you have rhubarb. Place the rhubarb and sugar in a large pot, add a small amount of water to prevent scorching, and bring to a simmer. Rhubarb releases a lot of water as it cooks and has a tendency to boil over. To avoid a sticky mess, use a pot much larger than necessary for the amount of rhubarb, leaving plenty of "head room" for foam to rise. Cooked rhubarb is often combined with strawberries to make pie filling.

Shallots *(Allium cepa var. aggregatum, Allium oschaninii)*

SEASON
Perennial

DEGREE OF DIFFICULTY
Moderate

CROP ROTATION GROUP
Roots Group

FERTILIZER
Balanced

CONTAINER GARDEN
Not recommended

DAYS TO HARVEST
Approximately 250

INTERPLANTABLE
No

Shallots are multiplier onions selected for flavor and keeping quality. They are either elongate and pointed on both ends, or round like a small onion. The flesh may be white or laced with purple, but the skin is always nut brown.

It is thought that shallots are native to Southeast Asia. They have made their way both east and west over the centuries, and are now eaten throughout the world.

Shallots can substitute for regular onions in a recipe, but are more often used where a milder, subtler flavor is desired. Add them to vegetable dishes involving asparagus, peas or mushrooms. Shallots are also an essential component of mignonette sauce, a classic accompaniment to raw oysters.

Planting

Where the growing season is short, shallots are typically planted in spring and harvested the following autumn. Where summers get hot and the season is long, plant shallot bulbs in fall, at the same time you would plant daffodils in your area. Press the bulbs, without removing the skin, into deep, rich soil, leaving the top $^1/_2$ inch (1.25 cm) protruding above the surface. Work a few tablespoons of bone meal into the planting area before you begin. Cover the bed with 2 inches (5 cm) of loose mulch, such as straw. Depending upon your location, foliage should emerge in late fall and overwinter or will appear in early spring soon after planting.

Shallots can be induced to grow in a large container but their productivity is limited at best. They will, however, tolerate light shade and can be planted in an area of the garden that might not be suitable for other crops. You can include them in ornamental plantings where the fat, blue-green stems add interest.

Cultivation

During the growing season, keep the bed free of weeds, and fertilize once in May and again in July, using a balanced organic fertilizer. Remove any flower spikes as you notice them to force the plant's energy into bulb production. Shallots begin to form bulbs as days are lengthening. Like other members of the onion clan, they need an inch of water a week. When tops begin to turn yellow, stop irrigating.

Harvesting

Harvest shallots in late summer when the tops begin to die back. Each bulb will produce several more. Replant the smaller ones the following fall or spring, depending upon your location. Allow freshly harvested bulbs to cure in a shady spot for a few days, until the foliage is dry above the top of the bulb. Spread them out on newspapers and protect from rainfall. When they are thoroughly dry, carefully remove soil and the foliage and store in a warm, dry, and dark place.

Shallots keep well in storage, but for convenience they can be peeled, chopped, and frozen in small portions. Whole shallots can be pickled like pearl onions, and sliced shallots can be preserved successfully by drying in a food dehydrator.

Strawberries *(Fragraria x ananassa)*

SEASON
Perennial

DEGREE OF DIFFICULTY
Easy

CROP ROTATION GROUP
Fruits Group

FERTILIZER
Balanced

CONTAINER GARDEN
Yes

DAYS TO HARVEST
1 year

INTERPLANTABLE
Yes

Strawberries can all be classified as one of three varieties:

June-bearing strawberries produce a single crop in early summer.

Everbearing (or day-neutral) strawberries produce a bumper crop in early summer, another smaller crop in late summer, and a few berries in between.

Alpine strawberries bear small numbers of fruits more or less continuously.

All strawberries adapt well to container culture, or may be grown more conventionally in beds. Alpine strawberries may struggle in hot, humid regions. Container-grown plants, however, have the advantage of being mobile. When the weather heats up, you can relocate them to afternoon shade.

Planting
Regardless of the variety, strawberries should be relocated every five years. Repot container-grown plants in fresh, sterilized mix annually. Doing so prevents a plethora of disease problems. Strawberries also should be separated by five years from soil that has previously grown any member of the tomato family. Hence their inclusion in the "Fruits" crop rotation group. Several important crop diseases are common to strawberries and the tomato clan, including potatoes, peppers, tomatillos, and eggplant.

Strawberries require full sun and well-drained sandy soil with a pH of 6.0 to 6.5. Rainfall or irrigation should provide 1 to 2 inches (2.5 to 5 cm) of water per week during the growing season. Prepare the bed by amending the soil with a 2-inch layer of compost over the entire area, well worked in.

Purchase certified disease-free plants in late winter or early spring. Everbearing cultivars are planted in hills spaced about 1 foot (30.5 cm) apart. June-bearing strawberries are planted in wide rows with plants 18 inches (45.75 cm) apart. Alpine strawberries are smaller and more compact than their cousins but are grown in the same way as everbearing strawberries. They need only 6 inches between plants.

Individual plants can also be grown in large containers. Use at least a 12-inch (30.5-cm) diameter pot for each plant. Any good commercial potting mix will work fine.

Cultivation

After the berries are picked, renovate the bed by removing old foliage and unwanted runners and adding compost. Properly maintained beds may produce for five years, although the first year will always be the best one.

Side-dress June-bearing cultivars with compost after harvest. Feed everbearing cultivars after the fall harvest. Do not add excessive nitrogen or you will encourage the growth of foliage at the expense of flowers. For container-grown plants, more regular fertilization will be needed due to the flushing of the container with water. Watering with soluble fertilizer every other week will keep plants productive.

Harvesting

Strawberries grown in beds should yield about $1^{1}/_{2}$ pounds (680 g) per square foot. A container-grown plant yields about 1 pound (454 g) per plant per season.

Strawberries can be frozen or made into jam or preserves. Rich in vitamin C and phytochemicals, fresh strawberries can be added to salad or turned into a cold fruit soup. They also star, of course, in desserts.

Strawberries

Culinary Herbs

We were tempted to place this section at the beginning of the book, because often a pot of herbs on the windowsill is the food gardener's first attempt at growing anything. This group of edible plants ended up at the end of the book because many, if not all, of them can be tucked into corners, grown in containers, and even moved indoors during colder months. Herbs are universally useful, and no garden should be without a few of the gardener's favorites. Even a relatively tiny spot can accommodate several varieties.

Herb gardening should not be an afterthought, however. Include them in your garden plan. Herbs assist with pest control in small gardens, because they are generally pest- and disease-free themselves and can help protect other plants from insects. With the exception of ginger, which is a root crop, all herbs can be considered leaf crops for purposes of crop rotation. Perennial herbs should be given a spot or container where they can remain undisturbed.

Garden-fresh herbs are a delight to the cook and among the most costly items in the produce department at the grocery store. Although dried herbs can substitute in some cases, many of the choicest herbs—basil, chervil, cilantro, and parsley, for example—lose their flavor with dehydration and are best enjoyed fresh.

Perennial herbs adapt well to containers and can be grown year-round, even in locations with harsh weather, if one has a sunny indoor space. Oregano, rosemary, and thyme are excellent choices.

We also discuss two tropical herbs, lemongrass and ginger, that grow vigorously even in climates as cool and cloudy as Great Britain.

The 15 varieties of herbs discussed should satisfy the repertoire of most skilled cooks. Where appropriate, tips are given for the best ways to use them in the kitchen and to preserve flavor after their growing season has passed.

Basil

(Ocimum basilicum, O. basilicum var. purpurascens, O. sanctum, O. citriodora, O. americana)

SEASON
Warm

DEGREE OF DIFFICULTY
Easy

CROP ROTATION GROUP
Leaves and
Flowers Group

FERTILIZER
Low nitrogen

CONTAINER GARDEN
Yes

DAYS TO HARVEST
60-70

INTERPLANTABLE
Yes

Basil, with its rich, clove-like aroma, was first cultivated in India about 5,000 years ago. Basil is technically a perennial, but is grown as an annual where cold weather occurs. When the mercury drops below 38°F (3°C), the leaves develop black spots and begin to drop. Species of wild basil have been hybridized for centuries and the resulting offspring, selected for desirable qualities, has created numerous cultivars. These varieties, all of which require the same care, include the typical green-leafed, clove-scented types and others that have lemon, lime, or anise notes. Compact, small-leaved forms, often known as *Greek basil,* are suitable even for the tiniest container gardens.

Cultivars designated as Thai or Asian usually have a stronger anise flavor than the varieties generally associated with Mediterranean cuisine.

Basil is a great choice for interplanting with other crops because it does not make heavy demands on the soil, and its essential oils offer some protection from pests, while the flowers attract pollinators.

Planting

Sow seeds in small pots about a month before you wish to transplant them. Transplant to the garden after all danger of frost has passed and the soil is warmed up. Beginning about two months after transplanting, the plants can be harvested periodically all season. The soil should be fertile, suitable for other vegetable crops, but need not be high in nitrogen. The plants must receive 1 inch (2.5 cm) of water per week or they may become rangy and leaf production will diminish.

Cultivation

Pinch off flowers to keep the plant producing. Regular harvesting keeps the plants bushy and productive. Feed with a balanced organic fertilizer about every three weeks during the growing season.

Harvesting

Harvest the plants by cutting off the topmost 6 to 8 inches (15.25 to 20.5 cm) of a stem. Immerse cut stems in a vase of water as you would cut flowers. Do not refrigerate. If left at room temperature for a week or so, they will root. Transplant them into the garden (or to 12-inch [30.5-cm] pots) when the roots are about 2 inches (5 cm) long, and keep well watered until the plants resume growth. This is a good way to extend the growing season into cooler weather, although the plants need bright light to grow well indoors.

Dried basil loses much of its flavor. Combining basil with fat increases its storage life significantly. Mixing minced basil with softened butter is one approach, or you can prepare an Italian-style pesto sauce. Either of these freezes well.

Chervil (Anthriscus cerefolium)

SEASON
Cool

DEGREE OF DIFFICULTY
Easy

CROP ROTATION GROUP
Carrot Family

FERTILIZER
Balanced

CONTAINER GARDEN
Yes

DAYS TO HARVEST
60

INTERPLANTABLE
Yes

Chervil tastes like a cross between parsley and tarragon, and its lacy foliage is decorative enough for the ornamental bed or pot. Because of its tolerance for cold, chervil can be grown throughout the winter in mild-winter areas. It withstands temperatures down to 4°F (-16°C).

Chervil is a member of the carrot family that originated in the Caucasus region. Roman conquerors spread the plant throughout Europe. It has become so associated with French cooking that it is sometimes called *French parsley*.

Planting

Sow seeds in small pots in late winter for spring planting or in late summer for a fall crop. Germination is slow, typically requiring about two weeks. The seeds look like small bits of black wire. Cover them as thinly as possible with a sprinkling of vermiculite, sand, or fine soil to prevent washing them out of the pots when irrigating. Keep plants well watered and in bright, indirect light. Chervil grows very well under artificial light. It is therefore an excellent candidate for out-of-season production indoors.

When the plants are 6 inches (15.25 cm) tall, transplant to the garden or to larger containers. A 12-inch (30.5-cm) pot is sufficient for growing a single plant to maturity.

Unlike most other herbs, chervil prefers to grow in light shade and will tolerate deeper shade. It can, therefore, be tucked into areas of the garden that might not be suitable for another food crop. Its lacy, decorative foliage blends well with ornamental plantings.

Cultivation

Fertilization is usually not needed in average garden soil. Feed container-grown plants every two weeks with a liquid fertilizer solution. As the weather warms up, the plants will flower and produce seeds. Seeds may be saved for the next sowing.

Harvesting

Clip the stems with scissors as needed. You can begin harvesting when the plants are about 1 foot (30.5 cm) in height, and continue all season. Take the entire leaf, clipping it off near the crown. This maintains a tidy appearance and prevents partially-cut leaves from yellowing on the plant. Use fresh-cut chervil the same day. It will keep, if the cut ends of the stems are immersed in water, for about three days at room temperature.

Chives *(Allium schoenoprasum, A. tuberosum)*

SEASON
Perennial

DEGREE OF DIFFICULTY
Easy

CROP ROTATION GROUP
None

FERTILIZER
Balanced

CONTAINER GARDEN
Yes

DAYS TO HARVEST
60-90

INTERPLANTABLE
Yes

If you are going to have only one member of the onion family in your garden, this is the one to choose. Chives grow easily in any well-drained garden soil in full sun to partial shade, producing tubular, onion-flavored leaves. If grown in full sun, the plants will produce flowers that are attractive and edible. Common chives produces pink pom-pom-like flowers in spring, while garlic chives blooms in fragrant, flat-topped clusters in late summer. Both adapt well to container cultivation. Common chives responds well to artificial light and can be grown year-round in containers.

Common chives is the only member of the onion family that occurs naturally in both the Old and New Worlds. They have been cultivated and eaten for at least 5,000 years and in various cultures have been used medicinally.

Garlic chives originated in Asia and is found in dishes from Korea to India. The plants have been naturalized in some regions and in a few areas are considered an invasive pest. Their spread is easily controlled by removing the flowers before they have a chance to produce seeds. They are excellent cut flowers.

Planting

Grow either species of chives from seeds, following the instructions for growing green onions. Started plants are available at most garden centers in spring. Once established in your garden, the clumps can easily be divided in spring to increase your supply. Simply dig, separate into several smaller clumps, and replant. Plants should be dug and divided every two years to renew the clump and keep them producing flowers.

Cultivation

Apart from regular watering, chives need little attention from the gardener. They will grow in poor, heavy soils as well as more fertile, enriched sites. Remove all flower stalks from garlic chives to prevent self-sowing, which can occur abundantly when conditions suit the plants.

Harvesting

Clip off individual leaves with scissors as needed. Flowers intended for consumption should be harvested just after they have opened. Cut flowers for the vase when they are fully open.

Garlic chives can be blanched to tone down the flavor and make them more tender. To do this, surround newly emerged foliage with a rolled-up newspaper or cardboard tube to shield out the sun.

At the end of the season, cut all foliage to the ground. This will result in more vigorous regrowth the following spring.

Preserving an abundant harvest of chives requires a little effort, as the dried leaves lose much of their flavor. You can prepare a compound butter as described for chervil, or you can place small amounts of chopped chives in an ice cube tray, add water, and freeze. When the cubes are frozen, turn them out into a re-closeable plastic bag and store in the freezer. Remove a cube or two to flavor soups or cooked potatoes. Freezing without the ice will result in mushy chives when they are thawed.

Cilantro *(Coriandrum sativum)*

SEASON
Cool and Warm

DEGREE OF DIFFICULTY
Easy

CROP ROTATION GROUP
Leaves and
Flowers Group

FERTILIZER
Not required

CONTAINER GARDEN
Yes

DAYS TO HARVEST
45-60

INTERPLANTABLE
Yes

In the United States, cilantro is often associated with southwestern cooking, but the plant is native to a wide swath of the Old World, from Southern Europe all the way to China. It is perhaps the most universally used herb in the world. All parts of the plant, from seed to flower to root, are edible. Cilantro stems and roots are essential to Southeast Asian curries. The leaves garnish everything from chicken tacos to *banh mi*, and are used in abundance to create the South American condiment *chimichurri*.

Cilantro seeds are often called *coriander,* and are a component of dishes as diverse as Jamaican jerk and kosher dill pickles.

Cilantro will tolerate considerable warmth but grows better during the cool season. In temperate climates, it will grow all season long. Where summers are hot, grow cilantro in partial shade.

Planting

Soak seeds in water overnight before sowing them where the plants will grow, or sow a few seeds in each of several small pots. Make successive plantings a week or two apart in order to have a continuous supply all season. Transplant the entire clump to the garden, or use one or two plants as part of a mixed container. In many areas of the world, cilantro is capable of establishing itself and need not be replanted each season. Leave a few plants to go to seed, and look for new seedlings the following season. Establishing a patch of cilantro is a good way to use a corner of the garden that might not accommodate other crops.

Cultivation

Keep cilantro irrigated, unless rainfall provides 1 inch (2.5 cm) of water per week. Fertilization is not necessary for plants grown in the ground. Containers should receive a liquid fertilizer about every two weeks. Remove weeds from the growing bed to reduce competition. Cilantro can also be grown out-of-season under artificial lights. Providing sufficient illumination is the chief restriction on producing cilantro indoors without a greenhouse. Fortunately, even young seedlings have intense flavor. Indoor crops can be harvested early and replanted, rather than trying to grow the plant to maturity.

Harvesting

Harvest cilantro by pulling up the entire plant, roots and all. Shake off the soil. Do not wash the foliage until just before you are ready to use it in the kitchen. Cilantro will keep a few days if stored in an airtight container with a damp paper towel.

If grown in containers, cilantro leaves can be harvested a few at a time and the plants will regrow. When the plants appear exhausted, tip them out of the container, remove the soil, and use the entire plant to make curry.

Cilantro leaves do not hold their flavor when dried. For long term preservation, allow the plants to form seeds, then harvest the coriander, which will keep in the pantry for months. Cut individual flower heads with mature seeds. Place them upside down in a paper bag and hang the bag in an airy place to allow the seeds to mature and dry thoroughly. Separate the seeds from the bits of stem and store them in an airtight container.

Dill *(Anethum graveolens)*

SEASON
Warm

DEGREE OF DIFFICULTY
Easy

CROP ROTATION GROUP
Leaves and
Flowers Group

FERTILIZER
None

CONTAINER GARDEN
Yes

DAYS TO HARVEST
60-70

INTERPLANTABLE
Yes

Dill is a warmth- and sun-loving plant and does not do well when summers are short or cool. If grown in shade, performance decreases dramatically. Gardeners in areas that are marginal for dill production will need to content themselves with foliage, as blooms are unlikely.

The tall, fern-like foliage of dill belies its relationship to other members of the carrot family, and its bright yellow flowers held in lacy umbels at the tops of the stalks make a bold statement in the late summer garden. Spring-sown dill will have foliage ready to clip about the time you dig the first new potatoes, and the two make a delicious combination.

Left to flower, dill attracts beneficial insects and provides seeds for flavoring pickles, salmon, and other foods. Compact forms that produce lots of foliage are best suited to container gardens, whereas the tall, seed-producing types do better if grown in beds. The slender stalks and airy foliage allow dill to blend well with other crops, and its small demands for water and nutrients offer little competition. It is therefore an ideal herb for interplanting.

Dill is an annual, but self-sown seed will return year after year where the climate is favorable. Dill can be interplanted with okra, as the two have similar soil and moisture requirements. It also grows well with cucumbers and other members of the squash family. Growing a few dill plants with your onions will deter onion fly.

Planting

Dill prefers well-drained, sandy soil with moderate amounts of organic matter. Fertility is usually not an issue, although container-grown plants will need some feeding during the growing season. Wait until after all danger of frost, and scatter the seeds where you wish them to grow. Other than watering, if necessary, you can leave them alone until harvest time.

Cultivation

Feed container-grown plants with liquid fertilizer solution every two weeks, as regular watering will leach nutrients from the pot. Plants being grown in the garden need not be fed, although if interplanted they will not be affected adversely by fertilization of their companion plants. Dill is sometimes preyed upon by caterpillars but otherwise is left alone by insects. The caterpillars that do attack are generally the larvae of the black swallowtail butterfly. They seldom do severe damage, and most gardeners leave them unmolested.

Harvesting

Harvest leaves as you need them, beginning when the plants are about 2 feet (61 cm) tall. If flowers or seeds are desired, harvest lightly until flower buds form then take all you want. The foliage keeps only a few days with refrigeration. Its flavor can be preserved by combining with softened butter and freezing the resulting compound butter, tightly wrapped in plastic or foil.

Dill flower heads can be harvested when the seeds have begun to turn brown. Clip off the entire head and place it upside down in a paper bag. Hang the bag in a dry, airy place to allow the seeds to ripen and dry out. When a few seeds fall from the head when you shake the bag, the flowers are dry enough to use in the kitchen. Dill foliage can also be dried using an electric dehydrator or a very low oven, and keeps its flavor well after drying.

Ginger *(Zingiber officinale)*

SEASON
Warm

DEGREE OF DIFFICULTY
Moderate

CROP ROTATION GROUP
Roots Group

FERTILIZER
Balanced

CONTAINER GARDEN
Yes

DAYS TO HARVEST
250-300

INTERPLANTABLE
No

Ginger grows from the fleshy rhizome sold in grocery markets as ginger root. You can simply purchase a piece to start your own clump. The plant is a tropical perennial, originating in southern China. Today, it is cultivated throughout the world in warm temperate to tropical climates. It is an essential ingredient in a wide range of Asian cuisine but has joined the European culinary repertoire in sweet dishes such as gingerbread and ginger ale.

Planting

Choose a plump, healthy-looking specimen with numerous eyes like potatoes. The best time to plant is in late winter. Select a container at least four times larger in diameter than the length of the piece of rhizome you are planting. Fill the container three quarters full with a good, well-drained potting mix containing plenty of compost. Place the rhizome on top of the mix with its eyes pointing upward. Cover with more potting mix and water well. Place the container in a plastic bag in indirect light until green shoots appear, which can take a month. Then remove the bag and water well. Keep the plant in bright, indirect light and never allow the soil to dry out. Growing plants need protection from wind and should be brought indoors any time the temperature is headed below 50°F (10°C). The ideal growing temperature is 75° to 85°F (24° to 29°C).

Cultivation

After all danger of frost has passed and the soil is well-warmed, transplant the container-grown ginger to rich, moist, well-drained soil in full sun. Feed every three weeks with a soluble organic fertilizer. After the weather heats up, the plants will grow rapidly. You can expect the clump to reach about 18 inches (45.75 cm) in diameter, and up to 3 feet (.9 m) in height.

Harvesting

Harvest ginger when the leaves begin to turn yellow. A plant started in a pot in February will be ready to harvest sometime in September. You can expect about 2 to 3 pounds (1 to 1.5 kg) of rhizomes from each clump. Gardeners with the ability to start plants as early as November and hold them indoors until spring will be rewarded with a much larger harvest. Dig up the rhizomes, cut the stems back to about 1 inch (2.5 cm), and spread the harvest in a warm, dry place for a few days to allow the skin to toughen and cure. The color will change from yellow-green to tan. Store the cured rhizomes is a cool, dry place. Ginger may also be dried, frozen, pickled in brandy, or candied.

Ginger may also be harvested when young, much as one would do with new potatoes. Probe carefully in the soil at the base of the plants with your fingers, scraping gently to expose the tender, pinkish rhizomes. Cut away a portion and replace the soil. Baby ginger can be sliced very thin and eaten as a condiment or added to stir-fry dishes.

During the growing season, you may also harvest a few of the plant's leaves. They can be used to flavor soup stock or tea.

Lemon Verbena *(Aloysia triphylla)*

SEASON
Warm

DEGREE OF DIFFICULTY
Moderate

CROP ROTATION GROUP
None

FERTILIZER
Balanced

CONTAINER GARDEN
Yes

DAYS TO HARVEST
120

INTERPLANTABLE
Yes

Native to western South America, lemon verbena was brought to Europe by Spanish and Portuguese explorers in the seventeenth century. Lemon verbena possesses an intriguing flavor, predominantly of lemons, but with interesting floral undertones. It is not reliably hardy outside frost-free areas, but can be overwintered indoors if you have a warm, sunny spot for it. It is quite adaptable to container growing. Because it is semitropical, lemon verbena does not grow well in cool-summer regions.

Besides its culinary uses, lemon verbena has long been used medicinally, and has been shown to have antibiotic activity against the pathogenic yeast *Candida albicans*. It was so valued as a medicine that the Spanish attempted to prevent other countries from obtaining plants or seeds, in order to maintain a monopoly on its production during the eighteenth century.

Planting

Lemon verbena seeds are difficult to germinate and slow growing. The flavor of seedlings varies, also. Therefore, it is preferable to obtain plants of known quality that have been propagated by cuttings. Purchase started plants from a garden center in spring and move outdoors after all danger of frost. Either locate the plants in a

garden bed, or place in a container at least 18 inches (45.75 cm) in diameter. If you intend to overwinter a plant, root cuttings in a glass of water in late summer, and pot them in small pots to hold indoors during cold weather. Warm, dry air from central heating encourages aphids and spider mites and makes overwintering a challenge without a greenhouse.

Cultivation

Keep the plants well watered, and feed every two weeks with a balanced organic fertilizer. They will grow into shrubs about 3 feet (91.5 cm) in diameter. After two or three months, tiny white or pale lavender flowers will appear at the ends of the branches. At this time, the plants will have the most essential oil present in the leaves, and therefore the strongest flavor.

Lemon verbena, when grown outdoors and given sufficient moisture, is seldom bothered by pests. Even snails and slugs leave it alone.

Harvesting

You can begin to harvest at about half the mature size, but do not take too many leaves at once. As the glossy, bright green plants are quite decorative, many gardeners wait until the end of the season and harvest most of the leaves at once. They retain flavor exceptionally well when dried; use either an electric dehydrator or a low oven. Just place on parchment paper on a baking sheet and dry for two to three hours in your oven, set to the lowest possible setting. Leave the oven door open.

Home-dried leaves will keep their flavor for months. The leaves wilt almost immediately after picking, so they are rarely used fresh or as a garnish. Use either fresh or dried leaves for tea, or steep them in sugar syrup for a dessert topping. Lemon verbena also makes a delicious herbed jelly. A well-grown, mature plant will yield enough leaves for drying, syrup, and jelly, so you can experiment to discover which you prefer.

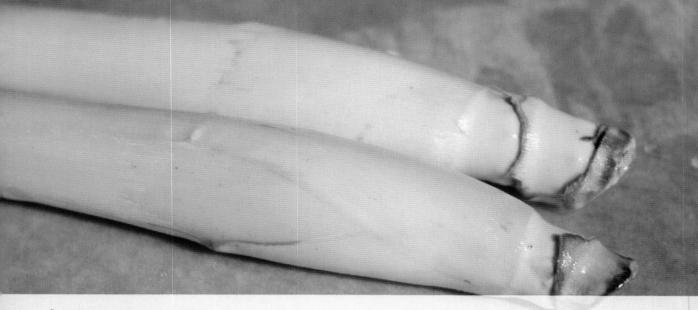

Lemongrass *(Cymbopogon citratus)*

SEASON
Warm

DEGREE OF DIFFICULTY
Easy

CROP ROTATION GROUP
Leaves and
Flowers Group

FERTILIZER
Balanced

CONTAINER GARDEN
Yes

DAYS TO HARVEST
60-90

INTERPLANTABLE
No

Lemongrass is a tropical perennial. It is also an essential ingredient of Asian curry pastes and soups. Its exact origin is uncertain, and its current range includes much of the warmer portion of the Old World. Plants found growing on Pacific islands were undoubtedly brought there in antiquity by seafaring humans. Because it needs a large container for its prodigious root system, starting over each year is recommended, as opposed to overwintering indoors. You can expect plants to reach over 3 feet (.9 m) in diameter with about five months of growth. Each clump produces dozens of usable stalks, so it is unlikely that the home gardener will need more than one plant.

Planting

Lemongrass can be grown from seed or plugs purchased at a specialty nursery, or can be started from stalks purchased at an Asian grocery store. Visit the grocery store in early spring to buy new starts. Lemongrass is sold as stems with most of the foliage removed. Each stem has a bulbous base. You may see tiny roots or root buds sticking out from the base. When planted, the basal portion quickly roots. Simply insert the stem about 1 inch (2.5 cm) into a small pot of damp soil mix, supporting it with a wooden stake. Keep the pot well-watered. Roots will quickly form.

When new roots protrude from the drain hole in the pot, you are ready to transplant outside, but wait until all danger of frost has passed and the weather is warm. If the plant must remain indoors for an extended period, transplant to successively larger containers as it grows. Lemongrass is tough and forgiving and does not mind frequent transplanting.

Cultivation

Lemongrass grows with amazing speed in full sun and rich, moist soil. Plants should be fertilized regularly with liquid fertilizer solution. Choose a balanced organic blend, and give each plant about a gallon of solution, prepared according to the package directions. The ideal growing temperature is 75°F during the day and 60°F at night. Lemongrass frequently inhabits boggy or flooded soils. For this reason it is impossible to overwater.

Harvesting

A full-grown clump of lemongrass will yield dozens of fat stalks. Wear heavy gloves and a long-sleeved shirt to protect your skin from the sharp, serrated edges of the leaves. Select stems whose base is about $^1/_2$ inch (1.25 cm) in diameter, and cut away from the main clump with a sharp knife. Trim the stalk to 8 or 10 inches (20.5 to 25.5 cm) in length. Stems will keep well under refrigeration for a week or two, or you can chop and freeze them.

Another approach is to trim individual stalks to fit a tall freezer-safe container. Pack them in vertically, alternating between "fat end up" and "fat end down," and it will be easy to remove individual stalks later as you need them. Lemongrass can also be dried successfully. Lemongrass flavor can be extracted with sugar syrup and used to flavor everything from tea to ice cream.

Mints (*Mentha* species and hybrids)

SEASON
Perennial

DEGREE OF DIFFICULTY
Easy

CROP ROTATION GROUP
None

FERTILIZER
None

CONTAINER GARDEN
Yes

DAYS TO HARVEST
60-90

INTERPLANTABLE
No

Mint refers to a complex group of plant species and hybrids, the majority of which do not come true from seed. About 15 species (botanists disagree on the exact number) are found throughout the world in temperate, wet habitats. Gardeners are advised to purchase cuttings struck from known cultivars.

Always taste mint plants before you buy, to make sure you get the flavor you want. Besides the typical peppermint and spearmint, you will find lemon, lime, apple, and cinnamon flavor variations, and more. In areas where the temperature does not fall below zero, mints are perennial. In cooler regions, they need to be started anew each season.

Planting

Mint is child's play to root, so you can purchase a bunch at the grocery store and produce multiple plants. Strip the leaves from the bottom half of the stem, recut the lower end of the stem at a 45-degree angle and set in a glass of water in a sunny window. Roots will form in a couple of weeks. Transplant the stem to the garden when the roots are 2 inches (5 cm) in length, after all danger of frost. Mint also adapts easily to container culture. Provide organically rich, but well-drained soil that retains moisture. Mint will grow in standing water.

Choose the garden spot for mint with care. Most cultivars will spread invasively and do not make good companions for other herbaceous perennials. Grow them at the base of large shrubs or trees, where they can spread luxuriantly. This will result in huge, sweetly flavored leaves.

Cultivation

Mints grow best in constantly moist to wet soil in partial shade. Try growing them in a mixture of sand and compost kept constantly moist. Soil that is too rich will produce rampant, straggly growth, small leaves, and an unpleasant flavor. Mint will grow out-of-season under artificial light, but it may be troublesome to keep plants confined to containers of convenient size. Take cuttings and repot regularly to keep them within bounds.

Mint varieties easily cross with each other, and the flowers are highly attractive to pollinators. As a result, seedlings will display a range of flavors if you grow different varieties near each other and allow them to self sow.

Some mint cultivars produce spikes of reasonably large, tubular flowers that can be picked individually and used as a garnish to flavor vinegar.

Harvesting

Begin cutting leaves as soon as the plants are large enough to tolerate it, after about four weeks of growth in the garden or container. The plants grow with amazing speed after the weather warms up and can be harvested as often as you like without damage. Mint leaves retain their flavor when dried, and the flavor can be easily extracted by steeping the leaves in sugar syrup. Combine 1 cup (236 ml) of sugar with 2 cups (472 ml) of water in a saucepan. Heat until the sugar dissolves, and let simmer for one minute. Remove from the heat and drop in 1 ounce (28 g) of fresh mint leaves (about 1 cup [236 ml], loosely packed). Allow to steep for half an hour, then strain and store the syrup in the refrigerator.

Oregano, Greek *(Origanum vulgare var. hirtum)*

SEASON
Perennial

DEGREE OF DIFFICULTY
Moderate

CROP ROTATION GROUP
None

FERTILIZER
None

CONTAINER GARDEN
Yes

DAYS TO HARVEST
60-90

INTERPLANTABLE
No

Naturally found in the warmer areas of Europe and along the Mediterranean coast, oregano has been cultivated for centuries. Human intervention has resulted in numerous varieties and forms with different growth habits and flavors. Greek oregano is a selection with fine culinary qualities. Always purchase plants of known provenance. Oregano can be grown by itself in a container, but its habit may overwhelm companion plants. It is easily established in the garden where winter cold does not fall below zero. This plant is a good choice for growing indoors in a sunny window, where its flavorful leaves will be available all winter.

Some varieties of oregano are sold for their ornamental value only and are not intended for cooking. While these can be an attractive addition to any garden, they are not the same as culinary oregano.

Planting

Nurseries that specialize in herbs sell started oregano plants grown from proven stock. More frequently, you will be offered seedlings. Because seed-grown plants may vary in terms of their culinary qualities, vegetatively propagated plants are better. If you are considering a purchase, taste a leaf to be sure you get the flavor you expect. Culinary forms also have thicker leaves, borne more densely on the stem, and thus yield a larger harvest from a smaller area.

The best source for culinary oregano may be the grocery store. Start cuttings in water as described for mint. When they are well rooted, transplant to 4-inch (10-cm) pots. When they are about 6 inches (15.25 cm) tall, move to the garden or to a large container. Oregano plants hug the ground and spread vigorously.

Cultivation

Provide lean, well-drained soil and hold off on the irrigation. "Lean" soil is low in nitrogen and organic matter. Sandy soil with a moderate amount of compost is sufficient. Keep the plants in full sun. If your plants bloom, delay harvesting, as the flavor will be impaired. Enjoy the blooms, which can be used as a garnish or in a vase. Then cut the plants to the ground to allow them to regenerate. Out of bloom, keep them clipped back and they'll keep producing leaves all season long.

Oregano is a suitable ground cover to plant along with other Mediterranean herbs.

Harvesting

Cut fresh leaves any time you need them for the kitchen. You can begin harvesting when plants are small, because they are so vigorous. Greek oregano retains its flavor well when dried. As spring merges into summer, oregano stems cease creeping along the soil surface and begin to grow upward in preparation for blooming. This is an ideal time to harvest them in quantity, as the long, straight stems are easy to strip. Place the leaves on a baking sheet lined with parchment paper and set in a warm, dry place. Alternatively, bind several stems together with a rubber band and hang them in an airy spot. Dry until the leaves crumble when crushed with your fingers, then store in an airtight container away from light.

Parsley *(Petroselinum crispum)*

SEASON	All
DEGREE OF DIFFICULTY	Easy
CROP ROTATION GROUP	Leaves and Flowers Group
FERTILIZER	Nitrogen
CONTAINER GARDEN	Yes
DAYS TO HARVEST	60-70
INTERPLANTABLE	Yes

Parsley originated in southern Italy, and on the other side of the Mediterranean in North Africa. In mild-winter areas, parsley will overwinter to provide both late and early crops from the same fall-planted patch. By succession planting, beginning in early spring, you can have parsley available any time. Italian, or flat leaf, parsley has the most intense flavor. Curly varieties look pretty on the plate and are just as nutritious as the flat leaf type.

Planting

Place seeds in a small container and cover with warm tap water. Allow to sit overnight. The next morning, strain through a tea strainer and return to the container, again covering with warm tap water. Repeat for three more days. On the fourth day, the seeds are ready to sow. This procedure will reduce germination time by two weeks or more. You can also plant seeds directly in small pots. Enclose in a plastic bag and place in the freezer overnight. Remove and keep moist. This also hastens germination.

Sow seeds thinly in small pots and grow under artificial lights if the weather is cold. They grow slowly, and will be ready to transplant to the garden when they are 6 inches (15.25 cm) tall. You can begin transplanting around the frost-free date in your area. Successive plantings can be made from spring through late summer, depending upon winter temperatures.

It is not advisable to germinate parsley in cell trays and then move the seedlings to larger pots before transplanting to the garden. Parsley develops a remarkably extensive root system. If the roots are disturbed more than once, this can lead to flowering during the first season, after which the plants may die. Blooming plants also develop a harsh flavor.

Cultivation

Parsley requires nitrogen to keep the leaves dark green and the plant productive. Side-dress the plants with cottonseed meal or another nitrogen source when they are about 8 inches (20.5 cm) tall, and then every two weeks during the harvest season. Plants need plenty of water but will rot if the soil remains too wet during cool weather. Root rot manifests itself as the entire plant wilts and collapses without warning. The only remedy is to replant, preferably in a new location.

Mulch to keep the soil cool and deter weeds. In hot-summer areas, the plants should receive afternoon shade. Parsley adapts well to container culture, and this may be the best way to grow it where climate conditions are a challenge. It also performs well under artificial lights.

Parsley is a good candidate for growing in an area of the garden that receives too much shade for other crops.

Harvesting

Cutting parsley either too frequently or too early may cause the plants to go to seed. Grow multiple plants and rotate your harvest among them. Cut only as much as you plan to use that day. At the end of the season, you can cut parsley back and preserve some of the harvest. Dehydrated parsley takes on the flavor of lawn grass, but minced parsley can be combined with butter to produce a sauce that freezes well.

Rosemary *(Rosmarium officinalis)*

SEASON
Perennial

DEGREE OF DIFFICULTY
Easy

CROP ROTATION GROUP
None

FERTILIZER
Balanced

CONTAINER GARDEN
Yes

DAYS TO HARVEST
90-120

INTERPLANTABLE
Yes

Rosemary has been flavoring roasted meats with its pine-like fragrance for centuries. It is also said to improve memory function. The woody stems with their stiff blue-green, needle-like leaves can be mistaken for a conifer until the sky-blue fragrant flowers are produced, usually in late spring. The fragrance is also pine-like.

As is the case with other Mediterranean herbs, the essential oils in the plant's leaves are responsible for the fragrance. In the wild, these oils probably help to fend off predators, and they do not readily evaporate under the hot sunshine. For the cook, this means these herbs retain much of their flavor when dehydrated, no doubt accounting for their longstanding endurance as a pantry staple.

An ideal plant for container growing, rosemary is equally at home in an herb bed. Most cultivars will tolerate only a few degrees of frost, so the plants are perennial only in mild-winter areas. There are prostrate forms that look good cascading over the edge of a pot or growing bed. These tend to be less cold-tolerant than the upright types.

Planting

Rosemary is difficult to grow from seed, and seedlings exhibit considerable variation in flavor, size, and frost tolerance. Therefore, it is best to purchase plants propagated by cuttings from known cultivars. This is especially true where the cold-tolerant cultivars are desired. Rosemary can be started from cuttings from the grocery store as described elsewhere. While cuttings will root in a glass of water, better results are to be had with damp sand, enclosing the cutting and pot in a plastic bag to maintain humidity.

Cultivation

Mix ground limestone with your regular potting mix or add it to the growing bed. Use about a cup of limestone per 100 square feet (30.5 square meters). Grow the plants in full sun, and do not allow them to dry out completely. A wilted plant may not recover. On the other hand, soggy soil will rot the roots and lead to rapid decline. For best results, do not mulch the soil around rosemary plants. If you desire a mulch for decorative purposes, use one that won't decompose and increase the water retentiveness of the soil, such as gravel.

Harvesting

Cut sprigs as they are needed for the kitchen. Rosemary is one of the best herbs for container cultivation and takes so well to pruning that rosemary topiary regularly appears for sale. Where plants survive winter, they will produce lovely blue, edible flowers in late spring. Leaves stripped from the stems can be dried, but if possible keep a plant growing indoors as the fresh flavor is superior.

At the end of the summer growing season, well before the first frost, prune off about a third of a container-grown plant, shaping it as you desire. Feed with a balanced fertilizer and then place it in a partially shaded spot. Water normally. When night temperatures become cool, move the plant to a sunny spot indoors. Reduce watering and feeding during the winter months and maintain good air circulation. Wait until the soil is almost dry before watering. Plants treated this way should remain in good condition all winter and can be returned to the outdoors for another season of growth.

Sage *(Salvia officinalis)*

SEASON
Perennial

DEGREE OF DIFFICULTY
Easy

CROP ROTATION GROUP
None

FERTILIZER
Balanced

CONTAINER GARDEN
Yes

DAYS TO HARVEST
90-120

INTERPLANTABLE
Yes

Sage will survive winter temperatures down to -25°F (-32°C). It is native to the Mediterranean region but has escaped from cultivation in some places and established itself. Culinary sage should not be confused with the sagebrush of western North America, which is an unrelated species (although the aroma is similar).

Culinary sage plants are decorative and can be used as the centerpiece of an herb bed or mixed container. The crinkled, blue-green leaves are about 1 by 3 inches (2.5 by 7.5 cm). Variegated forms are available, but they are more decorative than flavorful. A dwarf form appears from time to time in garden centers and is well worth growing if you can find it.

Planting

Transplant sage in early spring, as soon as the ground can be worked. Purchase started plants of known varieties from a garden center. Seedlings will vary in flavor, hardiness, and other characteristics. When in doubt, use the sniff test. Sage has an oily, savory aroma that should never be harsh or chemical. Poor-quality plants can smell like creosote. Set plants in average garden soil. Fertility is not important, but drainage is essential. Adding a tablespoonful of balanced organic fertilizer to the planting hole will supply the plant's needs for a season. Thereafter, feed lightly in spring as foliage emerges, again with a balanced formula fertilizer. Overfertilization will produce rangy growth and harsh flavor. While the best growth is obtained in full sun, sage will grow successfully with only six hours of sunshine.

Cultivation

Water only as required to keep the plants from wilting. Sage is remarkably drought-tolerant. Sage can also be grown in a container and moved indoors for the winter. It does not seem to mind the warm, dry indoor air of centrally heated homes. It does become quite large, however. A healthy plant may be 3 feet (91.5 cm) in diameter.

Fortunately, sage responds well to pruning, which is best done in early spring, as the plants are about to produce new growth. Cut back old stems to leave a plant of the shape and size you desire. Cuttings whose bark remains green and soft are easily rooted. Strip off most of the lower leaves, cut the stem at an angle, and stick the cutting into a pot of damp sand. Keep the sand moist and you should have a rooted plant within three weeks.

Container-grown or indoor sage plants need good air circulation to avoid fungal problems. Do not crowd containers. Indoors, a small fan blowing away from the plants is effective.

Harvesting

Begin harvesting leaves about two to three months after transplanting. Established plants can be harvested throughout the growing season. The leaves retain good flavor when dried, and are typically harvested in abundance at the end of the season. Sage is a traditional flavoring for many types of meat dishes, especially sausages.

The true-blue blooms of sage are also flavorful and can be used to decorate salads, garnish a plate or to flavor vinegar. They appear periodically on well-grown plants.

Tarragon *(Artemesia dracunculus var. sativa)*

SEASON
Perennial

DEGREE OF DIFFICULTY
Moderate

CROP ROTATION GROUP
None

FERTILIZER
Balanced

CONTAINER GARDEN
Yes

DAYS TO HARVEST
60-90

INTERPLANTABLE
Yes

Genuine French tarragon cannot be produced from seeds because its seeds are sterile. Seed purported to be for tarragon will most likely yield *A. dracunculus*, or Russian tarragon, which is not as desirable for cooking.

Planting
Purchase rooted cuttings or start your own from 6- to 8-inch (15.25- to 25.5-cm) stems from the grocery store, as described previously. Provide lean, well-drained soil that is slightly alkaline, and a hot, sunny location. Avoid peat and pine products in the growing mix. For container cultivation, choose a container holding about 1 cubic foot (30.5 cubic centimeters) of growing medium. Mulch with gravel. Mix a small amount of balanced organic fertilizer into the growing medium.

Cultivation
Above all, avoid overwatering. Tarragon is subject to numerous fungal diseases that thrive on excessive moisture. If you are successful in meeting its needs, a well-grown plant may be easily divided every two years. Just break apart the root mass and replant the clumps immediately. Tarragon is a poor candidate for indoor cultivation, as it is difficult to provide sufficient light. In locations where summers are long, hot, and humid, tarragon will not thrive.

Harvesting
Clip sprigs as soon as the plants have grown large enough, about 1 foot (30.5 cm) tall, in spring. Regular harvesting all season does no harm and results in bushy, vigorous plants. Tarragon may be dried for later use, or the flavor may be preserved in vinegar.

Mexican Tarragon *(Tagetes lucida)*

In areas that are too hot and humid for French tarragon, this marigold is an adequate substitute. The bright yellow flowers look good in bouquets and taste like tarragon, too. It is also known as *Spanish tarragon, Mexican mint tarragon,* and *winter tarragon.* Plants can be found in garden centers in hot-summer regions, or seeds can be purchased online.

Planting

Mexican tarragon thrives in full sun in lean, well-drained soil. Purchase started plants in spring and transplant to the garden after all danger of frost has passed. Alternatively, sow seed directly where the plants are to grow around the frost date, and thin to stand about 1 foot (30.5 cm) apart when true leaves have developed.

Like all marigolds, Mexican tarragon is easy to start indoors from seed if you can offer sufficient light. Sow seeds in cell trays three weeks before the last spring frost, keep them about 70°F (21°C), and provide good air circulation.

Cultivation

Good drainage is essential, and the plants are drought-tolerant. Performs best in soil with average moisture and fertility, suitable for other annual flowers.

Harvesting

Flowers or leaves may be harvested for the kitchen when the plants are about 18 inches (45.75 cm) tall. They will bloom lightly in spring and then heavily at the end of the season. Plants are usable all season long.

SEASON
Warm

DEGREE OF DIFFICULTY
Easy

CROP ROTATION GROUP
None

FERTILIZER
Balanced

CONTAINER GARDEN
Yes

DAYS TO HARVEST
45-60

INTERPLANTABLE
Yes

Thyme
(Thymus vulgaris, T. vulgaris var. citrosa, and others)

Thyme is perhaps the most useful of the culinary herbs of the Mediterranean region. It was cultivated by the ancient Egyptians. Today, hybridization and selection have provided us with numerous varieties to select from.

Look for French thyme, which produces long, straight stems from which the leaves are easy to strip. Various other thymes, representing several species and hybrids, are also available. Of these, the most useful in the kitchen are lemon- and lime-flavored forms. Other thymes are more useful for their decorative rather than culinary value, but their flowers are edible and can be used as a garnish or added to salads. Among these are several types of creeping thyme, which are best used as ornamental plantings.

Planting

Thyme grows under conditions similar to those favored by oregano and marjoram. Lean soil, moist but well-drained, and plenty of sunshine will give the best results. Cuttings from the grocery store are easy to root. Select the freshest, healthiest looking bunch you can find and strip all the leaves from the bottom two thirds of the stem. Trim $1/2$ inch (1.25 cm) from the lower end of the stem. Cuttings will root in a glass of water, but for faster rooting, insert the cut end of the stem into a small pot of damp sand. Enclose the whole thing in a plastic bag to create a mini-greenhouse.

Watch carefully for mold. Should it appear, remove the plastic bag for a few hours, moisten the sand if it appears to have dried out, and then re-enclose the pot in the bag. Roots should form in about two weeks.

If you choose not to start cuttings yourself, purchase started plants of known cultivars to be sure you get what you pay for. Seedlings may vary in flavor and other characteristics. This has not prevented seed companies from offering the seeds, nor nurseries from offering seedlings for sale. If you are considering plants of unknown provenance, rely on smell and taste to determine if you should bring them home.

Cultivation

As with many other herbs, good drainage is essential for success. Otherwise, little attention needs to be given to the plants apart from irrigation during dry spells. Light fertilization in spring with a balanced formulation provides all necessary nourishment.

Harvesting

Sprigs may be cut for the kitchen at any season. After flowering in summer, shear the plants back to encourage fresh new growth for fall. In mild-winter areas the plants are evergreen and can be harvested all winter long.

Index